I'D SAY
"YES," GOD,
IF I KNEW
WHAT YOU WANTED

This book witnesses profoundly and broadly to my earliest and lasting learning about God: God is everywhere. The stories tell us of God's unique, loving guidance to individuals of many faith traditions. I am grateful to have a book which will help people of any religion or no religion, to open to God's unique way of working with them.
– Judi Morin, SSA, MATh, prison chaplain and community adult educator

This collection of ordinary people's experience bears powerful witness to God's presence in our lives, bringing wisdom and insight as we open ourselves to God's desire for us. As the pages unfold, the reader becomes aware of an inner inclination – perhaps God's own invitation – to bring into focus and to ask one's own life questions. In all of this, Nancy opens the way to deepening friendship with God. This book is indeed a welcome gift.
– Karen Dickey, minister with St. Aidan's United Church, Victoria

Also by Nancy Reeves
A Path through Loss:
A Guide to Writing Your Healing & Growth

NANCY REEVES PHD

I'D SAY
"YES," GOD,
IF I KNEW WHAT
YOU WANTED

Spiritual
Discernment

Northstone

Editor: Michael Schwartzentruber
Cover and interior design: Margaret Kyle
Proofreading: Dianne Greenslade
Cover artwork: Mary Southard, CSJ, Ministry of the Arts, Sisters of St. Joseph, La Grange, IL
    Cover art is available as a card through: www.ministryofthearts.org

Northstone Publishing acknowledges the financial support of the Government of Canada, through the Book Publishing Industry Development Program, for its publishing activities.

Northstone Publishing is an imprint of Wood Lake Books Inc., an employee-owned company, and is committed to caring for the environment and all creation. Northstone recycles and reuses and encourages readers to do the same. Resources are printed on recycled paper and more environmentally friendly groundwood papers (newsprint), whenever possible. The trees used are replaced through donations to the Scoutrees for Canada program. A percentage of all profit is donated to charitable organizations.

National Library of Canada Cataloguing in Publication Data
Reeves, Nancy Christine, 1952-
    I'd say yes, God, if I knew what You wanted
Includes bibliographical references and index.
ISBN 1-896836-46-1
    1. God – Will. 2. Spiritual life. I. Title.
BT771.3.R43 2001   291.4   C2001-910831-1

Published by Northstone Publishing,
an imprint of Wood Lake Books Inc.
Kelowna, British Columbia, Canada
www.joinhands.com

Printing 10 9 8 7 6 5 4 3 2 1

Printed in Canada by
Transcontinental Printing

DEDICATION

To Rev. Herbert O'Driscoll,
who came into my life for a school year
when I was age 15, and "practiced what he preached"
by showing me God's unconditional love and call to service.

Contents

PART 2

METHODS

ACKNOWLEDGMENTS

I am so grateful for the many people who gave generously of their time and energy to help me bring this book to birth. Without my many "co-authors" who agreed to have their stories made public, my editor, Mike Schwartzentruber, and all the other folks at Northstone, who enthusiastically embraced this book; labour and delivery would have been much more difficult. Due to space limitations, I will only mention a few old friends and new, who read the manuscript and gave invaluable feedback. Thank you to my life partner, Bob Brinton, Judi Morin, Karen Dickey, Linda Kavelin Popov, Patricia Loring (whose writings on discernment inspired me greatly), Jan Palsson, Flora Slosson Wuellner, and Gerry Ayotte.

INTRODUCTION

Incline the ear of thy heart.
FROM THE RULE OF ST. BENEDICT

How I discerned I was to write this book

From October 1999 to June 2000, I gave 95 talks throughout Canada for non-profit groups, teaching the material from my new book *A Path through Loss: A Guide to Writing Your Healing and Growth*. Even though the section on spirituality in that book is small, it became an increasing focus for questions and concerns. Issues about life's meaning and direction often come to the fore during times of trauma, stress, and loss.

Many of the spiritual seekers I encountered were unfamiliar with the wide range of practices people use to encounter God more deeply. As I explained about retreats, spiritual direction, various ways to pray, and a myriad other things, I wished there was an easy-to-read book outlining concepts and methods of discernment, clarifying the individual path to which the divine calls us.

There are many useful and inspiring books on methods of prayer, and methods individual faiths or denominations or individuals use to grow into a fuller relationship with God. No book, though, to give a multi-faith range of discernment issues and methods. It did not cross my mind that I was to write such a book. As well as the lectures and workshops across Canada, I had a busy psychotherapy practice and a family who was not seeing much of me.

In late spring, I read in the local paper that Ralph Milton, spiritual storyteller extraordinaire, would be in town giving some workshops on how to make stories from scripture live. I decided to attend his evening workshop, thinking I would learn something and knowing I would be entertained!

During the evening, Ralph had us do a series of individual and small group exercises centered on a story from scripture that each of us felt was our "favorite of the moment." Immediately, I thought of the Christian gospel story of Jesus' friend, Mary. As she sat at his feet, listening to him teach, her sister Martha came in from the kitchen, where she had made herself extremely busy preparing for this large group, who, at some point, would be hungry and thirsty. Luke says Martha was not only busy, but was "distracted by her many tasks" and complained to Jesus, "do you not care that my sister has left me to do all the work by myself? Tell her then to help me."

Martha expected Jesus to back her up. In that time and culture, it was not considered right for women to sit with the men, discussing spiritual and religious issues. She had tradition and law on her side. Jesus probably shocked everyone in that room by his radical response: "Martha, Martha, you are worried and distracted by many things; there is need of only one thing."

Jesus was always inviting people to let go of the small picture, our ego-imposed desires and "shoulds," to reach out for the big picture, a richer relationship with God. *All* faiths encourage this change of perception and suggest varied ways to move towards this goal.

During the evening workshop, Ralph asked each of us to sit quietly and turn inwards until we could see our chosen story. Mine began prior to Martha's appearance. As we placed ourselves in the tale, we were to turn to one of the other characters and ask a question. I didn't get a chance to do this. In the visualization, I looked to my right side and found Peter sitting beside me.

As our eyes met, he stated firmly, "This is not the place for women. You should be helping Martha." Out of my hurt feelings, I responded, "But I want to listen to him."

"I will tell you later what he says."

"That's not good enough, I want to hear directly."

As I continued dialoguing with Peter, I felt more confident that this was "right" for me.

After a few minutes, Ralph asked us to step out of our visualizations and tell our story to our small group. After each person had a chance to do so, Ralph spoke of the importance of taking scripture personally, if we are to help these words live for others.

As the evening was drawing to a close, Ralph threw out a simple question which exploded deep inside me with the feeling of importance I associate with a message from the Spirit. He said, "You might want to look at how your chosen story reflects an issue in your own life, right now." Immediately I received a flood of images of the times recently I have spoken of spiritual issues in public gatherings. Accompanying these images was a strong anxiety. Giving it words, it said, "Who are you to speak of spirituality to others? You are a psychologist; you have no degree in theology. People will laugh at you or be angry with you."

Two days later, sitting in prayer by my living room window as the sunrise warmed the sky, I revisited my story and "knew" that the way I spoke with others about spirituality fit within my mandate as a healer and helper. I was not telling others what to believe. I was giving them encouragement and guidance to find and follow their own path.

A warm, peaceful sensation grew inside, which felt like an internal sunrise. After a few minutes of resting in this experience, a thought moved in.

"A guidebook about discernment would be useful for people."

"Yes," I agreed, "I wish I knew of one."

"You could write one."

"You're kidding. I don't know enough."

Image of Mary, listening. "Okay, what gifts would I bring to such a book?"

I then saw a list of the following points:

- You cherish and are interested in learning about the diverse paths of other faiths and denominations.
- You have experience and skills in interviewing. It will be important to include many stories.
- You enjoy writing and have published books and articles.
- You are aware of the need for a book such as this and people are already asking you for this information.
- Personal healing, growth, and discerning the path you are called to, are priorities in your life.

"Um, pretty persuasive reasons," I respond. "What would the book be called?"

Right away I saw the title: *I'd Say "Yes," God, If I Knew What You Wanted*. I laughed myself into acceptance.

Speaking of lemons

Who would you rather have make the lemonade: you or God? How a person acts on the adage, "When life gives you lemons, make lemonade," can tell a lot about their relationship to themselves, to others, to the world, and to the Source of our Being. On one extreme are those who want to, or believe they *have* to, handle life alone. At the other extreme are people who believe that they are powerless pawns of a God who manipulates them for his or her own amusement, without caring for them.

There is a broad middle ground. Those who live here often have had some experience of Holy Mystery, something beyond themselves that *does* care. They may have experienced this many times or just once. It may have touched them during worship, while walking in the woods, or while looking into the eyes of their newborn child. During a time of confusion or pain, they may have had "just the right person," or book, or dream, or awareness, come to them, to clarify the path to healing or growth.

This book is for those who do not believe we live in a random universe. It is for those who wish to make lemonade with God. For, once we have been touched by this Higher Power, it is natural to ask, "What then would you have me do?"

Spiritual practices are relationship builders. Each person may have different goals when they seek to develop a stronger relationship with the divine. For example, you may be looking for one or more of the following from your spiritual practice:

- a growing sense of connection,
- deeper understanding of God's nature and presence in the world,
- healing for yourself or for others,
- transformation of blocks and restrictions that keep you from being the person you were meant to be.

You may also engage in a spiritual practice as a way to
- express love and gratitude
- listen for and clarify your role in the divine plan.

Although this book focuses on the last goal, discernment, the others are interrelated and some of the stories touch on them.

What is discernment?

Discernment is the process of clarifying and understanding God's will for us. Patricia Loring, a Quaker who has written a number of excellent books on discernment, describes it as "that fallible, intuitive gift we use in attempting to discriminate the course to which we are personally led by God in a given situation, from our other impulses and from the generalized judgments of conscience."[1]

Is belief in a Creator necessary for discernment? No. People walking spiritual paths, such as Buddhism, do not believe in a divinity. Discerning the path that will lead each person to right living and enlightenment is extremely important to Buddhists, however. And the Dalai Lama, the spiritual head of Tibetan Buddhism, speaks of the necessity of relationship.

> [I]t is just as important in Buddhism as it is in the Christian context that one's spiritual practice be grounded in a single-pointed confidence and faith, that there is a full entrusting of one's spiritual well-being in the object of refuge. In Buddhism, one's practice must be grounded in taking refuge in the Three Jewels – the Buddha, Dharma (the spiritual path), and Sangha (faith community) – and in particular, in the Buddha. In that relationship, there is not only a sense of entrusting your spiritual well-being to the guidance of the Buddha – a fully enlightened, perfected being who has fully realized the enlightened state – but you are also aspiring to realize that state within yourself.[2]

The Dalai Lama cautions, however, against viewing all faith traditions as the same. Each spiritual path has uniquenesses to be cherished. And deep understanding of a path is not possible without walking it for some time. Many spiritual seekers find that dialoguing with those of another faith tradition opens them to the wonder of diversity and encourages a fuller sense of gratitude and honoring of their own path.

The process of discernment assumes that we are trying to choose a path that leads to goals consistent with the divine urge to love, and desire for healing, growth, justice, and freedom. Some questions, such as "Should I rob this bank?" do not need to be asked. And yet, if that is your question, it is important to bring your concern to God to discern how to meet your needs: "I'm really worried about paying the rent now that I've lost my job. How do I find my way through this, God, when robbing a bank seems the only option?"

At times, we say we are following divine will or speaking for the divine, when we haven't included God in our decision-making process at all. Some people say those who divorce are breaking God's will, citing, from the marriage liturgy as "proof," "Whatever God has joined together, let no man break asunder." Did the married couple seek to discern God's will for them prior to marriage? Or was the desire for union based on hormones, or unexpected pregnancy, or a hope to find security, or a demand from parents or religion, or many of the other reasons our ego can give for acting?

God *may* have been saying, "This marriage is not a good idea," for years before one of the couple finally hears. The state of marriage is sacred and God calls many of us to it. But so is every other lifestyle that is life affirming. Just because a person has committed to a relationship, or vocation, or other way of being in the world, doesn't mean God has called us to it. Just because we make a commitment in God's name doesn't mean we are actually doing God's will.

If we are called, it may also not be forever. One woman told me that she received a very strong call to a particular four-year university degree program. In her third year, she started to feel an urge to switch to another program. She resisted for some time, remembering that her original decision had been based on some long and thoughtful discernment. When the urges did not leave, she opened her heart and mind to examining this new direction and found that it would use her gifts even more fully! She discovered that this new program had not been in existence at her university three years previously. She also realized that the three years of course work she had already undertaken were either prerequisites for the new program, or would give her knowledge base a broadness that would enhance her career. The original call was true. So was this one.

Will, longing, yearning

Some recent writing in the area of discernment uses the terms God's *yearning* or *longing*, instead of *will*. The authors say that these two words often reflect more clearly our Creator's attitudes and behaviors towards us. There is concern that the word "will" carries a connotation of demand or coercion.

In the *Theological Dictionary of the New Testament*, I discovered that the term used in the Hebrew and Christian scriptures is similar in meaning to yearning and longing. The Greek word *thelo* was used to translate the original Aramaic terms for divine will. *Thelo* has varied meanings: "to purpose," "to be ready," "to resolve," "to desire," "to wish," "to prefer." One of the emotional flavors of *thelo* is erotic: "to come together," "to conceive."

I have used "will" throughout much of this book. I invite you to use the terms that resonate most strongly with you.

Layout of the book

The first part of this book briefly explores concepts around discernment; the second part describes various individual and group methods that diverse faith traditions use to listen for God's will. Most of the concepts and all of the methods are illustrated with a story. I view these stories as pieces of colorful stained glass or mosaic, with the concepts taking the part of the leading or cement that unobtrusively provides a structure and direction.

Fifty-seven stories come out of interviews I have conducted over the past year. Twenty-one further stories have already been published in autobiographies or biographies of people such as Gandhi, Mother Teresa, and Jean Vanier. The stories reflect a wide variety of ways to discern divine will. As I chose stories to illustrate different concepts, I realized that without the name of the person and identifying information, you would not be able to tell which experience had been lived by Ada McKenzie or Paul Taylor, and which was the story of C. S. Lewis or Teresa of Avila. God does not save the "really good stuff" for certain people.

The storytellers

The most frequent question people asked when they discovered I was writing a book on discernment was, "How did you find enough people to fill a book?" Actually, it was much easier than I ever thought it would be. In fact, I now believe that in any room containing 100 people, and I don't just mean clergy or other religious folks, there would be enough stories to write a sequel.

As I related examples of the stories I had collected, my questioners would often pause thoughtfully and then respond, "You know, I had an experience some time ago. It was awesome and I haven't known what to make of it." I would then hear another wonderful story about being guided to the right decision or path. Some of these stories ended up in this book.

Talking about our past "God-touches" often changes how we perceive our personal history. John English, a Jesuit who has written a number of books including *Spiritual Freedom*, speaks of our "graced history." He says, "A series of events becomes graced history when it is approached and understood in terms of God's constant loving presence with each individual and the whole human race."[3]

Most of the people I meet in my psychotherapy practice have survived a traumatic experience. The first telling of their story is often completely negative: pain, fear, feeling alone in an uncaring world. As their healing progresses, it is interesting to see that their story often changes. The facts usually remain the same. What is different is the stress they place on certain aspects of the experience. Instead of concentrating on the nurse who was brusque and who didn't seem to care, the healing person speaks thankfully of the paramedic who held her hand throughout the trip to the hospital.

As you read the stories in this book, you may find yourself re-membering your past differently. This can sensitize you to the holy in your life and clarify how God has called you to discernment.

In order to include as wide a range of faith traditions as possible in this book, I searched out some of the participants. Many others found me, after discovering my interest. I interviewed most people in person, but a few by telephone due to their distance from me. Their stories were recorded on audiotape or by my own brand of shorthand. Rarely was the first draft of the written story accepted as is. To ensure that I had faithfully captured the essence of the story, it would pass back and forth between us until my storytellers said, "That's got it!"

Talking about the profound God-touches in our lives is an intimate experience. Many of the people I interviewed said discussing their sex lives would have been easier. As they shared their personal stories, however, we discovered that the telling did not just benefit me. Some participants said they had never spoken their story out loud before, or hadn't seen it as a logical progression of events until they talked with me. I received many telephone calls in the weeks after the interviews, from storytellers who thanked me for the experience. Here's a small sampling of comments.

- "The interview started me looking at the history of my spiritual path, and I realized that there were many other times Spirit has guided me."
- "After talking to you, I have felt a deep awe all week about this Loving Creator, who wants me as partner. I thought my method was pretty ordinary until I spoke it out loud."
- "I could see that I am currently wondering about whether to go back to school or travel. And I was trying to figure it out myself. Since the interview and this subsequent realization, I have entered an intentional discernment process."

All the stories in this book are certified to be true by the ones who told them. They are not all factual. I changed facts that would have identified those who wished to remain anonymous. I tried to change information that would not affect the essence of the story. Sometimes giving the person another name and not identifying them with a particular religion was enough.

Variety of methods

Some of the discernment methods presented here will remind you of your own graced history. Others may intrigue you or invite you to sample them. A few may seem so foreign or weird that it seems unimaginable how they could be valid. But an infinite God can contact us in unlimited ways.

It is easy to misunderstand a discernment method if we look at it separate from its context. For example, historically, the rich holistic aboriginal spirituality of many different lands was usually seen as primitive, misguided, and/or evil, by European and Asian conquerors. Although a discernment method may be unfamiliar to us, if it is practiced by a particular religion or denomination, it usually has a long history of use, and probably developed in response to a divine call, taking many factors into account, including culture, level of technology, and spiritual practices.

God words

There are many names and phrases used to address or talk about the holy, including but not limited to Allah, Most High, Lord, Goddess, The All, The Boundless, Yahweh, Creator. If my storytellers had a preference, I used their choice. The words I tend to use most frequently are God, Holy Mystery, and Source of Being.

Allowing God to speak to you through this book

Many of the people who reviewed this book for me took longer than I expected to complete it. Each story can be read in a few minutes, so I anticipated the whole book would be finished in a day, or in a few evenings. I had not considered the richness of the material; one reader compared the stories to pieces of double chocolate cheesecake. If she didn't take time to savor and digest each story, she experienced a feeling of being overstuffed.

If your purpose in reading this book is to aid your own discernment process, give God time to speak to you as you read the stories, as well as afterwards, as you ponder them in your heart. You may find it useful to journal your reactions or to speak of them to someone you trust.

PART ONE

CONCEPTS

Let's make this personal

You are the deep innerness of all things,
the last word that can never be spoken.
To each of us you reveal yourself differently:
to the ship as coastline, to the shore us a ship.
RAINER MARIA RILKE[4]

I bring a number of presuppositions to this book. To begin, I believe that God wants a personal relationship with us and is constantly inviting us into intimate partnership. We have been given free will so the partnership is always invited, never coerced. No matter how "spiritual" we are, the experience of our relationship with Holy Mystery ebbs and flows. Sometimes we feel a deep connection; at other times, we may wonder if the holy has "skipped town," leaving us alone.

JUDITH'S STORY

Sometimes I feel like I'm alone in the wilderness as I'm trying to make a decision. I repeatedly ask God for a clear sign and nothing comes. I've had enough experiences to know, though, that God is working within and around me and that if I trust and keep walking the path that seems right for me, I will receive direct guidance as I need it.

A lot of God's guidance is indirect. The process of trying to decide whether or not to adopt a third child was very challenging. I swung between the peaks and valleys of "yes" and "no" many times. I put off signing the papers committing myself to my daughter Faarh until the last minute.

A week after sending the papers, I was re-reading information about my new daughter. I looked up her birth date in my journal to see what was going on in my life on that day. I read about being at Westminster Abbey retreat center for the week-end, something I did about once a year. That particular day I was praying for a child! The last niggling doubts about my decision vanished. This was my God-given daughter. I find that remembering those moments of clarity, when I know God wants me to take a certain path, sustain me during the dry wilderness times and the times of doubt.

By changing our question from "Is God with me?" to "How is God with me right now?" we are more likely to see the support and guidance that is being offered as we move through the ups and downs of life.

Grace

Grace adapts itself to each person. We make our choices,
some of which are good for us, some bad, and then grace shapes the results.
DEEPAK CHOPRA[5]

As we walk our spiritual path, evidence of God's lavish love for us becomes more and more evident. This awareness often results in the realization of our unworthiness to receive such a gift. This is true. And if God's love depended on our worthiness, no one would receive it. We are cherished for who we are, with all our shortcomings. This is grace.

We are not used to free gifts, with no strings attached. It can produce anxiety to know that we can't control God's grace. Even though we are repeatedly told that divine grace and love will never be taken away from us, we would feel more comfortable if we could ensure its continuation.

Father John Shea has written many poems and stories about this lavishly loving God. I heard one of his stories about grace on an audiotape. It concerns a fellow professor at the seminary where they both taught. Shea's colleague offered a course on grace. As you can imagine, the course left the students with a feeling of gratitude for this stupendous gift.

The feeling changed to consternation and anxiety, however, when they got the year-end exam. It was a killer. They all failed. As a body, the students approached the professor and complained. "Here you teach us about God's free gift to us out of unconditional love, and then you give an exam we all fail! This isn't fair!"

The professor responded that it was true that everyone had failed. The students thought they had been betrayed and continued with expressions of anger, pleading, and anxiety. Then the professor added, "You have all failed the exam; and I am going to give you all passing grades. This is grace." There was a stunned silence. Then the students were angrier than ever. They wanted to rewrite the exam. They did not want a mark they had not "earned." It is hard to accept grace. *grace is about acceptance accepting God's acceptance of us.*

Free will

*To live out of the living God
and not only out of our own resources and power
is an ancient religious passion.
To move in harmony with what is ultimately the case,
to ride the rhythms of God is the essence of salvation.*
JOHN SHEA[6]

Not only is God a God of relationship, we have been given free will so that our connection with the divine is both a gift we are given and a gift we *give*. There would be no reason to discern God's will for us if we did not have free will. For without free will, we would be puppets. Our free will is an indication that God deeply trusts us. Often we revel in our freedom, although in times of disaster and loss, we may wish the Holy would take complete direct control and rescue us in the way we specify.

C. S. LEWIS' STORY

C. S. Lewis, theologian and author of many fiction and non-fiction books on spirituality, including the Narnia series, spoke of his spiritual growth in *Surprised by Joy: The Shape of My Early Life*. He describes how he fought the idea of a supreme being, as he was simultaneously wooed by God. To this point, Lewis had always felt in control of his philosophy and kept it safely outside of himself.

Lewis conceived of God as a supernatural dramatist and felt that it would be impossible to have a personal relationship with such a Being just as a character in a book could never "meet" the author. Then two people he admired immensely for their commonsense attitude to life began to speak of taking God personally. Lewis was deeply shaken. He continues the story.

> The odd thing was that before God closed in on me, I was in fact offered what now appears a moment of wholly free choice. In a sense I was going up Headington Hill on the top of a bus. Without words and (I think) almost without images, a fact about myself was somehow presented to me. I became aware that I was holding something at bay, or shutting something out…I felt myself being, there and then, given a free choice. I could open the door or keep it shut; I could unbuckle the armour or keep it on. Neither choice was presented as a duty; no threat or promise was attached to either, though I knew that to open the door…meant the incalculable.[7]

As C. S. Lewis discovered, our Creator greatly desires a relationship of mutual consent and is exquisitely respectful of our right to say "yes" or "no." Saying "yes" does change our perception of the world and leaves us open to transformation. Lewis experienced this metanoia or "change of heart" as a melting of the "man of snow" he had been. Many others similarly discovered that it is often during a stuck or stagnant point in their lives that the divine call is clearly heard for the first time, frequently when they are doing something mundane, like riding a bus.

Benefits of intentional spiritual practices

Ask, and it will be given you; seek, and you will find;
knock, and it will be opened to you.
For those who ask receive, and those who seek find,
and to those who knock it will be opened.
MATTHEW 7:7–8

In any human endeavor, preparation smoothes the path. The prerequisites for smoothing the discernment process include having an intentional spirituality with spiritual practices, combined with some degree of self-awareness and right living. We'll get to self-awareness and right living in the next two sections, but first let's look at the importance of spiritual practice.

Imagine that you are a member of a group meeting to find solutions to a problem in your community. After a number of sessions, you become aware of a particular person in the group. You are very attracted to this person and want them to be your friend. You respect the way they handle themselves in the meeting, you agree with their comments, you appreciate their sensitivity and respectful manner towards others.

"I would like to be a friend of that person," you say to yourself. If you can believe the smiles and warm way the person greets you, it seems they would also like you for a friend. So you suggest a social contact and the response is a quick affirmative.

Now you have some decisions to make. Where to go? What to do? How long to be together? When to get together? If your goal is a connection that meets some of your new friend's needs and desires, the answers to these questions cannot be answered by you alone. Being in the group has given you some knowledge of your new friend, but not enough to generalize to a social contact.

It would be even more difficult to guess at the needs and desires of a stranger you are meeting for the first time. An intentional spiritual path with spiritual practices helps us grow in our knowledge of our God. We also become familiar with how the divine reaches out to us and learn which spiritual practices move us to deeper connection.

Waking up one morning, deciding to believe in God, and asking, "Okay, what would you like me to do?" might bring an answer. Without awareness and familiarity with the divine, we are more likely to interpret the answer in a rigid manner. Or we might look for a particular mode of answer and not hear the one we are sent – like looking under the streetlight for the keys you dropped in the middle of the road, because that's where you can see more easily.

A number of people have told me about their conversion experiences. A conversion experience is an encounter with God that is so intense and profound that the person feels totally new afterwards. "I was turned inside out and upside down." "I didn't know I was away from 'home,' until I experienced home in God." "It took my spirituality from a head level to a heart level in a split second."

The afterglow and aftermath of a conversion experience can last for a lifetime. Without a prior intentional spirituality or opportunity to talk afterwards with someone knowledgeable about conversion experiences, it is common for the recipient to view the encounter in a narrow, literal manner. One man told me that, for months, he only read Psalm 23, "The Lord is my shepherd…," because that is what he was doing when he was "hit out of the blue by God's love."

Francis of Assisi heard God tell him, "Go and repair my church which is falling down." He immediately started collecting stones and mixing mortar to rebuild the local church, which was in ruin. It was difficult for him, because he had no training or experience as a stonemason. Sometime later, St. Francis realized that God wanted him to walk a path that helped repair the Christian Church. He had taken the words literally.

If we don't see God's bigger picture, the Holy works with us to bring the most benefit for ourselves and for others out of our partial understanding. So manually repairing the little church was a healing and growing experience for Francis. God's will was still accomplished. If, however, Francis had spent the rest of his life rebuilding broken down churches and refused to mature in his ability to listen to the divine, he wouldn't have realized the broader role God envisioned for him.

BRAD'S STORY

I had thought I had it all together. Life was going the way I wanted. When I heard of others who got off track I thought, "Well, I'm above all that," and felt quite smug. Then I sinned and my brokenness was in my face. It wasn't just a mistake; it was a fracturing of my relationship with God, others, and myself. As I struggled with the shock of this reality, I felt alone and adrift. What do I do with my life now? What path should I take? That first week of hard thought was invaluable to me because I realized that it would not be possible to discern what course to take in my life until I had the prerequisites. The sin had to be addressed. I needed to admit my guilt to myself, others, and God. Then I needed a process of reconciliation, of repairing that fracture.

It couldn't be done alone. I needed to allow God to transform me. The fracture had happened in the first place by relying too much on ego. I had thought of myself as a "good" person and had made the assumption that I was not like others who were weak and, therefore, sinners.

That first week was like a wake-up call. I prayed a lot. Out of that prayer time came the awareness that, after admitting my guilt, I needed to develop a number of spiritual practices to become more aware of my connection to the Holy One. Since I was very clear that the rest of my life needed to be in partnership with God, time would need to be taken to deepen this relationship.

I began to attend worship services faithfully. I spent more time with others I felt were God-centered, sometimes asking them to help clarify issues or problems. Individual, daily prayer became deeper and richer. Journaling my path allowed me to see how God was working in my life.

In time, it became easier to hear the difference between Spirit speaking within me, and my ego's voice. My ego, which I called "The Editor," was loud and brazen. Spirit, on the other hand, spoke in a still, small voice. No wonder I hadn't heard this before. I hadn't taken the time to really quiet myself and listen.

As I became more used to listening to Spirit, I found another sign. During decision-making, I would often experience a spine-tingling sensation as I contemplated one path. For a moment, the hairs on my body actually stood up! This was the way God wanted me to go. As I acted on that decision, I would continue to experience the tingling at times, although subsequent sensations were much less intense. If I got off track, and was "listening," I felt a little niggle inside.

After some years of this spiritual reconnecting, reconciliation, and practice of discerning God's will for me, I felt ready to ask some bigger questions. I'm now in the process of deciding on a career. The direction is coming clearer and I don't want to rush it. It's often hard for other people, though, who ask me, "Now that you're out of prison, what job are you going to get?"

I remember back to that first week in solitary confinement after I turned myself into the police and was charged with second-degree murder. There were many tortured thoughts: What kind of person am I that I could kill the wife I love? How can I ever repay this crime? How could God still love me? How could I ever love myself again? How could I ever be accepted back in society, and be safe?

And yet it was during that time that I turned again to God and was guided to the path of healing. I knew I needed to give my whole self to God. Someone told me recently that John Shea, in his book *An Experience Named Spirit*, speaks about two kinds of judgment: God's judgment is for possibilities; people's judgment tends to be for shame. The difference between restorative and punitive justice. I knew prison would be rough. There would be many rules I would need to follow; some of them would make no sense.

I decided during that week of solitary confinement that I would obey the people laws by entering into a covenant with God. I vowed to God that I would live my prison term as a monk: in poverty, obedience, and chastity. This was also what my keepers demanded of me. By covenanting with God, I felt I would take these people demands to a higher level. This vow helped me through my long sentence.

I read Romans 7 and 8 frequently. Statements such as, "For those who live according to the flesh set their minds on the things of the flesh, but those who live according to the Spirit, set their minds on the things of the Spirit" (Romans 8:5), gave me a direction. This I have tried to follow throughout my prison term and beyond. Nothing I can do will bring my wife back to life. With God's help, though, my life is being transformed, and I hope now to be a force of healing in this world.

NANCY'S STORY

Looking back, Nancy realizes that there was about a year of preparation before God told her directly and clearly what to do. Over that year, Nancy found herself more consciously including a faith perspective in her psychological counseling practice. She also experienced her worship experience becoming richer, more fulfilling.

One day, I suddenly felt a compelling urge to get away and pray. I'd never felt anything like that before. It was like a strong fountain gushing up inside me and I knew it was asking me to move into a space of silence. The urge continued until I arranged a three-day, undirected silent retreat.

It was during Advent and it truly felt like a time of new birth for me. On the last day of the retreat, I had another first-time experience. God spoke to me, audibly, clearly. "I want you to become a priest." My automatic response was, "You've got to be nuts!" Ordination was something I was not considering. Although I was now an Anglican, my background was in a Christian denomination that had no clergy. I was just getting used to my new church. Now God wanted me to be ordained!

I went into shock. For the next six months I struggled with this call. When I said my "yes" to God, I then entered the structured discernment process of the Anglican church. This was very helpful, especially the questions that were given to me along the way. The specific direction and implications of my call became clearer and fit more easily.

Now, ordained as a Deacon in the Anglican church, my work life is divided between a large pastoral counseling agency and duties at a parish church. The diaconate is a ministry which is rising again within the church. As Ormande Plater says, it is like living on the razor's edge. We bring the concerns of the community into the church and symbolize the church in the world.

My discernment method has become more frequent with time. When I have a decision to make, I trust that God will direct me. I try to be vulnerable to the fact that our life is not as simple as we would like it to be and wait receptively. I become more present, taking time to watch for the small miracles that occur all the time. If something seems to go wrong, such as a missed appointment, I look to see what God is doing with this situation.

Then, I may be in the middle of a social gathering and feel the fountain inside me calling me to silence. As soon as possible, I move into prayer and the issue becomes clearer. Sometimes I need to be in silence a few minutes, other times I feel the urge to make a retreat. When I feel the fountain, to be certain it's God's request and not my ego, I ask myself some questions: Is it time for a break or a rest? What is going on for me emotionally? If I discover that I have unmet needs, I honor them; if I don't have needs at the time, I move into prayer to wait on God.

Which spiritual practice will be most helpful on our life path? I believe that God invites us to the methods that offer us the healing and growth we need at any one time. If you don't hear a clear call, try a number of spiritual practices and be receptive to those that "feel right."

Benefits of self-awareness

The Query of Queries
Rabbi Zusya said, "In the coming world,
they will not ask me: 'Why were you not Moses?' They
will ask me: 'Why were you not Zusya?'" [8]

A second prerequisite for, or help to, discernment is self-awareness. Catherine of Siena, a 14th-century mystic, conceptualizes the spiritual life as a large tree. The tree has many parts, which support and nurture each other. The root of the spiritual life is *self-knowledge*. Self-knowledge brings nutrients into the core of the tree, which she sees as *patience*. Here transformation occurs. The energy that is produced feeds and strengthens the trunk, which is *love*. Love reaches out to the world through the branches of discernment.

Some level of self-knowledge makes it easier to determine if that inner voice or urge is from me or from God. My ego is the part of my mind where I react to and make meaning of the world within and around me. It tells me I am an individual and that it knows what's best for me.

Unfortunately, the ego often takes in information indiscriminately. Even with much contradictory evidence, if an authority figure tells me when I am a child, "You will never amount to anything," my ego takes this statement as truth. Unless and until I consciously examine this "truth" and decide it is not reality, I will continue to build my life around it. Even knowing intellectually that this message is false, it often takes time and energy to change my attitudes and behaviors that feed the belief.

Writers in spirituality speak of our essence or "true self," which is made in the image of God, and our "false self" ego or personality, into which we have taken lies about our nature and woven them into attitude and behavior patterns. Choosing to live out of our essence means being willing to confront the mask we wear to please the world. Since we are far from our essence, this confrontation brings the scary prospect of leaving the restrictive familiar for the wide open unknown.

Personal growth can come in many ways, including counseling or psychotherapy, reading self-help books, and attending workshops. A self-awareness procedure that is also used as a discernment method is the Enneagram. The Enneagram (pronounced ANY-a-gram) views each person as having one of nine personality types. Each type has its unique gifts and challenges. This system assists the process of personal awareness and growth by clarifying an individual's motivation, instead of just looking at behavior.

In *The Wisdom of the Enneagram*, Don Richard Riso and Russ Hudson state that it "is a condensation of universal wisdom, the perennial philosophy accumulated by Christians, Buddhists, Muslims (especially the Sufis), and Jews (in the Kabbalah) for thousands of years."[9] It does not advocate a particular type of spiritual path. By encouraging self-awareness, the Enneagram can aid discernment by helping us uncover our truth. Richard Rohr, OFM, has written *Enneagram II: Advancing Spiritual Discernment*. He says, "Our task in discernment is to sift through appearances and the many ambiguities of our life situations, and from among the various alternatives, decisions, or choices, to discover where the truth is."[10] The Enneagram is one of many tools that can assist this process.

YVON'S STORY

Raised as a Roman Catholic, I like to say that I quit going to church when I got to be taller than my mother, which was around the age of 14. I quit school a couple of years later, at 16, and joined the RCAF the following year. By the time I was 25, I had been married for five years and was the father of two young sons. I realized I had no skills or qualifications that would lead to success in the world, so I started back to school by taking a correspondence course at the grade 11 high school level.

Fortunately, someone I worked with encouraged me to apply to university as a mature student. (All I've ever needed in life is a little encouragement and it has been amazing what I've been able to achieve.) I was accepted. After six years of working midnight shifts and being a full-time student, I entered the business world.

Fresh from the success of completing a university degree I was determined to succeed in business. Good at motivating others to see my point of view, I often acted as the catalyst for change within the organization. I succeeded in the business world with apparent ease and quickly climbed the corporate ladder.

In my mid-40s I remarried and became a father again at 46. A couple of years later I was transferred yet again, but this time I realized it was time to put down some roots. I took two actions to begin establishing these roots. I announced to my corporate colleagues that I was not prepared to move again and my wife, Laura, and I started to go to church. I have come to realize that these decisions were critical in leading me to where I am today.

My decision not to move again spelled the beginning of the end of my corporate life. Within a couple of years, I had become uncomfortable with the corporate direction my colleagues intended for the company and I was not prepared to compromise my principles. This naturally led to a great deal of internal anguish and considerable self-doubt, which was fueled by the fact that I was well paid for the work I did.

At the same time, and even though I had become actively involved with the church, my spiritual life had not emerged. I recognize now that I was in spiritual trouble and ripe for transformation. I was not happy with my work life and had not yet committed to a new direction. I continually rejected suggestions from Laura that I read books on spirituality and personal growth, such as Scott Peck's *The Road Less Traveled*. I rejected her suggestions and would push her away. After all, hadn't I become a success on my own? I would tell her I didn't need anyone or anything. I had to solve my problems myself.

Then, one day when I came home from work, I heard some unfamiliar music playing. I must have been ready, because just like it did for Scott Peck, "Marilyn von Waldner's exquisitely penetrating melodies and lyrics met me at just the right point in my own spiritual journey." As it turned out, Scott Peck had written a book called *What Return Can I Make?* which is a collection of essays and meditations on passages of scripture and spiritual themes which were inspired by Marilyn's songs and heartfelt music.

I devoured Peck's books over the next months and began my spiritual journey in earnest. Church involvement took on new meaning for me and I looked for opportunities to explore my new sense of being. My first time in the pulpit on stewardship Sunday, the reading was from Paul's letter to the Romans: "Do not be conformed to this world, but be transformed by the renewing of your minds, so that you may discern what is the will of God, what is good and acceptable and perfect" (Romans 12:2).

The scripture spoke to me, as I wanted to do the pure and noble and perfect thing. I wanted to be transformed. But how? Shortly after this, my corporate life came to an end and I struggled with what to do next. I came across a book written by Lois Wilson in which she wrote, "I chose to participate in activities that engaged people with others and, therefore, had within them the possibility of lives being changed, of love being learned and expressed."[11]

This was it! This was what I longed to do. I thought that since I had let God into my life the most perfect career for me would be ministry. I wanted to work for God, and it had to be on the front lines. Shortly thereafter, I became a full-time student at Vancouver School of Theology, and a candidate for ministry in the United Church. Now I was doing the good and acceptable and perfect thing through the path I was taking.

Halfway through my second term at VST, the cancer diagnosis came. Our whole lives were turned upside down. I remember meditating in my hospital bed, as I anxiously waited for surgery. For the first time in my life, personal mortality stared me in the face. During the meditation, a very clear vision came to me. It was of a cup, more than full to the brim, for the liquid was running over in a stream. A "knowing" came with the vision: "You've been given so much. Why are you worrying about what you are supposed to do, just do it. No need to wait for the perfect time or the perfect place."

I wasn't sure what this knowing meant, although it seemed to be connected to the two quotes that had affected me so much. With the vision and words came a sense that I had no control over death. Instead of triggering my need for control, I felt relieved that this was God's area. As I lay in meditation, there was a deep sense that I was not going to die. With this sense came more words, "You've been given gifts; use them." As I thought about my gifts, I realized that administration was one of my strongest ones. This gift was being almost totally repressed in my new career path. I did not see it as compatible with spirituality.

It seemed that God wanted me to use this gift. How was I to do it? It was shortly thereafter that I was offered an administrative position at VST, which I accepted and fulfilled over the next six years. During this time I discovered the typology of the Enneagram. This new knowledge has been important in helping me to understand my life and the choices I have made. Eventually, I came to see that the Enneagram Type 1 description fit me best.

Among other things, it is important for Type 1s to do things right, to find the perfect path. We are also very practical. As I learned more about myself, I realized that my ego had been trying to control my path, rather than allowing God and my higher self to provide the direction. My ego's definition of perfection and rightness was narrow, so it seemed that the only acceptable path open to me was to be ordained. Once I allowed God into the decision-making, I began to see how my gift of administration could be used.

I discerned to receive my degree, without being ordained. Then I took a position as Executive Director of a local palliative care society, Surrey Hospice. I have been able to use my business savvy to make hospice much more visible in our community, so that the people who need our services can access us more easily. Knowing how to speak "business," I have developed relationships with a number of companies who donate funds for new projects we are offering. Recently, we secured funding to put on a series of free workshops, which over 600 people attended.

I have found the Enneagram extremely useful as a personal growth tool. Through it, I am able to be more aware of my life-enhancing and life-restricting tendencies. When I experience an urge towards or away from a particular path, it is easier to determine if the urge comes from God or from my ego.

BUDDHIST PARABLE

The only son of a wealthy man left home and fell into extreme poverty. He lost everything, even forgetting his parents. The father looked long and hard for his son, but couldn't discover his whereabouts. Decades later, the son wandered near to his former home. His father was overjoyed when he heard news of him and sent servants to bring his beloved child home.

But the son was overwhelmed by the idea of being heir to so much magnificence and wealth and could not believe the servants had found the right person. He thought he was being deceived and refused to go with them.

The father sent servants again, this time telling the son that there was a lowly job opening in the household. The son was pleased to have regular food and a place to live and gladly accepted the position. The father promoted his son as rapidly as the man would accept, until he became the highest-ranking servant, in charge of the whole estate.

At this point, as the father was nearing the end of his life, he called all his family and friends together. In his son's presence, the father told the gathering that all his possessions belonged to his only son, the man who still thought of himself as a servant. Finally, the son saw his true nature and rejoiced.[12]

Since we will continue to change throughout our lifetime, there will never come a point where we know everything about ourselves. Self-knowledge, as the root of our spiritual life, needs ongoing watering and fertilizing. Sometimes this "gardening" will be hard, yet it is worth the work, for our "tree" will bear the fruit of a deeper relationship with ourselves, others, and our Creator.

Benefits of right living

O Lord, my God! Assist Thy loved ones to be firm in Thy Faith,
to walk in Thy ways, to be steadfast in Thy Cause. Give them Thy grace
to withstand the onslaught of self and passion,
to follow the light of divine guidance.
Thou art the Powerful, the Gracious, the Self-Subsisting, the Bestower,
the Compassionate, the Almighty, the All-Bountiful.

ABDU'L-BAHA[13]

A third prerequisite for, or help to, discernment is right living. Throughout history, some people and religions have believed that the way to achieve spiritual growth is to negate or diminish one aspect of the person in favor of another. Usually it has been the intellect or the soul that is honored and the body and emotions, our "animal" aspects, that are judged inferior. This belief assumes that God gave us bodies or feelings by mistake or as punishment.

As soon as we prefer one aspect of our totality to another, we become unbalanced. For example, our bodies are "our temples" and give us important information about our needs and desires. It is through meeting these needs and desires that we often touch and are touched by the divine.

Abusing or ignoring an aspect of ourselves not only unbalances us, it also has a negative effect on the part we cherish. As students cramming for an exam can attest, our minds do not process information as quickly or as clearly when we are fatigued or undernourished. So cherishing all of ourselves as gifts of God will place us in the most conducive situation to heal past and present wounds, delight in our connection with the divine, and have the capacity to answer a call to service.

BILL WHITE'S STORY

I am of the Coast Salish people, born in Nanaimo. I work as Aboriginal Liaison Officer at the University of Victoria. In my job, I have been able to bring the wisdom of aboriginal people into academia. We have had some courses co-taught by professors and First Nations elders. Frequently, professors of courses ranging from child care to psychology, contact us to provide information for their students about aboriginal practices.

When my office is contemplating a new project, we include elders in the discernment and planning process. Elders bless our meetings and the new project. They provide suggestions based on traditional values. Sometimes the old people enter the room where we are meeting and immediately say they will not work with us. Our energy is not balanced. It is all right to have differing views, yet if the people in the meeting are not willing to listen to each other, there will not be a good outcome. The old people can sense this.

In 1855, Chief Seattle spoke about connections between our world and that of our ancestors by saying, "there is no death, only a change of worlds." It is these words that provide the context for the teachings of the elders and, through them, our interaction with the natural and supernatural worlds.

As a very young child, I recall seeing my parents listen intently when our grandfather lit a candle at the dinner table and then uttered words to the great Creator. After invoking a prayer or song, I also saw them listen intently as he charged them with the rules of good living. The old people stress the importance of great love for each other, of the importance of humility in the things that we do, and of balance within ourselves. Being able to apply such things ensures significant contact with each other, the ancestors, and the Creator.

My father died when I was five years old. My mother raised us with very strong traditional values learned from her parents and grandparents. I grew up during a time when aunts, uncles, and grandparents were very active in my growing, giving much love and a sense of security. Later, as an adult, I realized that the teaching I had been given prepared me to move from the place of self, of seeing myself as a separate entity, to a place of interconnection.

To be effective, any discernment process must work with all the energy: mental, physical, emotional, spiritual, that of ourselves, others in our world, the sacred. To do this, we need to find focus and balance. This stance has to be practiced.

One day I was feeling very rushed and, in fact, cranky. I didn't know how I was going to complete all the work I had that day. One of my "to-dos" involved telephoning an elder to ask him to take part in a meeting. I definitely knew I wasn't balanced, yet I thought I could cross another task off my list with a short phone call. This phone call had to be made by 10 a.m. before the elder moved to undertake his duties. Because of this time restraint, I felt even more rushed. It did not look good at all. The call had to be made or another series of problems would be created.

The elder, who I knew very well, answered the phone. I greeted him using our own language, "*e-chew-I-all Siem na Sulxwane*/How are you learned elder?" He responded that he was well and asked me the same thing. I replied, "*Estun-u-l-all Siem/* I am fine," and launched into my request. Partway through this conversation, I felt guilty because I was, in fact, cranky and had added to this by lying to him and doing so in our own language. It seemed he would know I was not telling the truth and that, if honesty were not forthcoming, I was not likely to be trusted.

I apologized and told him how I was really feeling. His response was, "You haven't eaten; you are hungry." In that flash of a moment, I thought about what he said, paid closer attention to my feelings, and realized that was the problem. I was hungry! Now, whenever I speak with him, I make sure that I have had something to eat.

Much of our traditional teaching helps the child learn to gracefully accept change. The old people who remember the rules associated with various states of change from one world to another (puberty rites, naming, initiation, marriage, death) always spoke about our connectedness to each other, how our people always moved together as a community. To ensure safe transition from one state to another, they brought forward prayers, songs, and advice to surround, to protect. It is through these actions that young people, who were trained to watch and to listen, would know what to do when it came time for them to move in front of the community.

Songs, prayers, guidance, and insight flow from the Creator to the ancestors. Some of this wisdom is ancient, some is given in this generation. There must be right living to hear clearly. If, for some reason, we are consumed by great sadness or pain, or by drugs and alcohol, then the transmission is interrupted. Chief Dan George said, "For some time bewilderment will, like an ugly spirit, torment you." This, in part, is why the old people, whenever they had a chance, asked us to "make our minds strong." They taught the importance of letting tears and sadness flow, but not to let such things consume who we were and, thus, damage who we might become.

If someone has moved away from right living, the prayers and ceremonies can be a way back to balance. If, as Dan George said, they let it happen. This was not easy for the old people and it is not easy for us. When we treat each other well, then the songs, prayers, and ceremonies bridge the worlds; and the energies of our ancestors and the Creator move amongst us one more time.

Our ancestors, the grandmothers and grandfathers, are always with us to provide support and guidance from the other world. It is their energy which forms part and parcel of our world, their world. One day in late winter, I heard my mother, who has passed on, say to me, "I'm standing with you every morning. Each day is a new day, every day is a day of transformation. With spring comes the blooming of flowers to remind us of the cycles of life."

It is important to learn to accept transformation because it is always connected with discernment. The Creator's will for us involves change and growth and if we do not allow this process, we will not become the people we are meant to be.

As a child, I heard the old people speaking of the ancestors who had lived before the coming of white people to our territory.

These ancestors were given visions of large puffing snakes, spewing flames and smoke from their heads, that would move across the mountains. They had foreseen the coming of trains to our lands. The ancestors also spoke about whales that would beach themselves, open their mouths and people would walk out. They saw the coming of modern ferries to our shores. To be able to integrate these visions without becoming unbalanced, the Creator gave us songs and ceremonies to provide a safe structure.

We are also encouraged to accept divine guidance with humility. And we are taught that the Creator is everywhere and in everything. Humility involves letting go of ego and being in awe of this sacredness around us. When transformation occurs out of a place of deep humility, we are emotionally prepared to pass through times which could be dark. Focus, balance and great love for each other, within the stance of humility, ensures movement through the place of darkness in a safe, reasonably quick, and long lasting way.

Right living nourishes our mind, body, and spirit, so that we are more receptive to the divine. If we allow it, any physical sensation, emotion, thought, or soul experience can open us to our Creator. A common experience of mothers nursing their infants is a deep sense of rightness and connection with their little ones, which soon expands to a feeling of interconnection with other mothers and babes, with all God's children, with all creation, and with our Mother Earth and our Mother God, the "Source of Our Being."

Obedience

We are in a love relationship with the Holy One,
not a manipulative liaison, not military obedience,
not sentimental whimsicality.
FLORA SLOSSON WUELLNER[14]

Saying about someone, "She's very obedient," may not be seen as a compliment. In today's world, the word obedient often conjures up images of a passive, spineless, dependent person who follows blindly because they can't think for themselves. So, does following God's will for us mean a return to a feudal mentality where we relinquish control to an arbitrary overlord?

PHYLLIS' STORY

Phyllis came to me recently to talk about her spiritual path. She said she had grown up with the teaching that God was a punitive father who demanded unquestioning, blind obedience. Punishment for any transgression would be swift and fierce. In the last few years, due to some experiences of God's deep unconditional love for her, Phyllis was opening to a new image of the holy.

She had been taught that she was to be unassertive with God, ignoring her own needs and desires. She prayed for others, not for herself. This attitude, as so frequently happens, generalized to other relationships. She became a doormat for other authority figures, never expressing her own wishes to parents, employers, or partners. This stance attracted those who had an aggressive approach to life and Phyllis found herself in abusive relationships.

Psychotherapy allowed Phyllis to change her attitudes and behaviors to an assertive stance. She could now clarify, honor, and seek to meet the appropriate needs and desires of others and herself. Her relationships became mutual. It was when Phyllis was receptive to mutuality in relationship that she could feel divine touches of love. This changed her image of God.

Phyllis brought me a question. "How can I explore this new assertive spirituality without throwing out all my past religious history? I have many role models for assertion outside of religion. I would like a spiritual role model for healthy relationships. When I look back at my religious education, all I can see are wimpy women."

"Can you think of any women from your faith tradition with whom you used to resonate?" I asked.

"Well, yes, it's embarrassing now to think about, though. I always loved Mary of Nazareth, yet she's the biggest wimp of them all. Meek, mild, blindly accepting God's will for her."

"Oh, you mean the Mary who stood up to an Archangel?" I countered.

"What???"

So I told her the following story.

The archangel Gabriel came to visit Mary of Nazareth. I imagine his unexpected appearance was pretty impressive. Yet Mary does not fall flat on her face before him. Gabriel begins by greeting her, telling Mary that she is favored and that the Lord is with her. Mary is very perplexed and confused by these words. Gabriel realizes this and speaks to put her at ease. It is not God's way to terrify or beat us into submission.

Gabriel tells Mary she needn't be afraid and continues with the astounding news that she, an unmarried woman, will shortly bear a son who will become a great king. Mary reminds him that she is a virgin and questions how this conception can possibly occur. Today, she would probably say something like, "You want me to do what?" When Gabriel answers her question, Mary responds with her "Yes": "Here am I, the servant of the Lord; let it be with me according to your word." Gabriel leaves.

Standing up to an Archangel and asking for clarification shows strength and good self-esteem. Obviously God is pleased with this attitude of assertiveness because Gabriel is very willing to answer questions.

Phyllis was stunned and agreed that she needed to re-examine stories from scripture, particularly the stories of women, with new eyes. There are many examples of creative, independent, assertive, faithful women and men in the scriptures of all faith traditions.

To be obedient is to be receptive. The root word, *ob-audiere*, means to "listen attentively." Diarmuid O'Murchu says authentic obedience "requires a radical and attentive openness to the deeper message and meaning of all that we are asked to attend to. Only in the light of such deep listening can we respond in a more wholesome way."[15] Because of the restrictive meaning the term obedience has for many, O'Murchu suggests those who wish to commit their lives to following God's will "rename the call to obedience as the vow for mutual collaboration." (O'Murchu, p. 88)

Mission Impossible

*Co-creation implies a still unfolding creation
in which the Creator continues to work with and through us
when we respond in faithfulness to the promptings
of Love and Truth in our hearts.*
PATRICIA LORING[16]

In the 1960s, *Mission Impossible* was a very popular television program in Canada and the United States. The show's original premise and title has also been used for two recent movies. The show's main character is Jim, a man who has the ability to bring together a team of people with exotic skills any time the world needs saving. And it needed saving every week in the 1960s.

Jim's chief (never seen) would make contact via a tape recorded message and inform him, "I have a mission for you, should you choose to accept it." Ah, free will! The chief went on to explain that if Jim were caught or killed, he would disavow any connection with or knowledge of him. Jim was on his own. He always said "yes," of course, and galloped off to save the world.

This is how some people view their relationship with God. They discern what the divine is calling them to do, they say, "Right, Chief, I accept," and then go off by themselves to "do it for God." Then, as they struggle along the path, meeting roadblocks, detours, and one-way streets going the wrong way, they rationalize the difficulty in a number of ways. "The straight and narrow is harder than the broad way." "God is testing me to see how committed I am."

Meanwhile, God is trying to get their attention. "Doing life alone truly is Mission Impossible. Let's work in partnership. Taking each step together allows you to receive my grace, support, and wisdom." Traveling the path intentionally with the Creator can result in a goal that looks very different from the original conception. God is supremely flexible, taking changing situations or circumstances into account. Trying to do it alone sets us up for failure. And it's not nearly as much fun.

Divinity loves diversity

I love it when we waltz

I love it when we waltz.
Held securely in your embrace,
swirling down and in.
Easiest for me to let go into you.

Then you begin to foxtrot.
I don't know this dance.
Let's go back to waltzing.
What if I step wrong?

How freeing, though, to know that if I follow,
I don't need to know where we're going
You danced all into creation,
you will dance me if I let you.

Then, I read about the rhumba.
Some swear it is the best dance to dance with you.
So I start to rhumba, but you don't follow.
Don't you want me to have this experience?

I feel your love stroking me, but I turn from you and pout.
Being wallflower is so lonely though,
I turn back and you dance your delight to rock and roll.
How often I forget, you always want what's best for me.

Sometimes you start a folk dance.
And I feel all the dancers as one
And I greet you in each new partner,
colorful diversity in joyful abandon.

Then my ego decides that you have all the good moves.
And I want to lead.
You move with me into the waltz,
and don't complain as I step on my own feet and yours.

There are many dances left to learn,
And you will teach me the ones I need,
to be the dancer I was meant to be.
Although the waltz is still my favorite.

Your Love makes my dancing lovely
Your Grace makes my dancing graceful
Thanks be to you, Holy Dancer.
NANCY C. REEVES[17]

If you were God, how many different types of fish would you have created? If you don't like fish, probably very few. Would you have allowed a process of evolution? As well as diversity in creation, there is diversity in paths to the divine. The range of religions and spiritual practices can look overwhelming to a new seeker. I liken this abundance to a really large buffet, in a restaurant known for nutritious and appealing food, that I am invited to attend whenever I want. If I try to eat everything, not only will I get sick, one taste will overlay another so that I can't truly appreciate the flavor of any one particular food item.

When I am first presented with the buffet, I will probably gobble quickly and overeat. As time goes on and I trust that the food will always be there, I become more selective. I start to anticipate and connect with the nuances of my favorite dishes. As I become familiar with the layout of the buffet, I am able to meet my hunger needs and desires more effectively. At times, a new food may call to me and I either incorporate it into my regular diet, or delight in it for a bit and then stop choosing it.

So it is with our personal spiritual path. God invites us to the path that meets our particular spiritual needs. We may have been born into our path and it fits us well for our entire life. Some of us discover that a different path will give the most opportunity for connection with God. Spiritual guides suggest that it takes time to learn about your path and to find the way to use it most effectively. Intentional, patient exploration is called for.

DOUG SEELEY'S STORY

I have a very strange gift. I consistently find four- and five-leaf clovers, even patches of them. At first I thought it was normal; after a couple of decades I noticed that it was a rather unique ability. With my background in synchronicity and Jungian psychology, I just could not understand what this ability was good for, or why I had it. It would take a couple more decades to find out.

It was as a boy that I started having peculiar experiences in which there were strange connections between my thoughts and what happened in the world. I would later know them as synchronicities. When I was a teenager, I became an atheist, although I read a lot of Taoism, Zen Buddhism, and psychology. I was also interested in Greek philosophy, especially pre-Socratic. They put forward their ideas about the First Principle of the universe: some said it was energy, others said water or air. But one, a certain Anaximander, said it was the "boundless." I did not know exactly why, but something deep inside me knew that this guy was right. His inspiration has stayed with me.

As a grad student at the University of Toronto, I did some studies with Marshall McLuhan. In one lecture, he spoke about the role of the I Ching, the ancient Chinese book of wisdom that has been used for divination for at least 4,000 years. Divination can be viewed as the discernment of how the entire universe evokes the present moment, with specific people in a specific place. In this lecture, he said that the I Ching had contributed greatly to the evolution of the human species. Although I had viewed this book as "merely" a source of folk magic, McLuhan's comment stimulated me to study it. It was then that I learned of Jung's interest in it and in what he called synchronicity.

So for a few years I used the I Ching to assist me to make difficult decisions. The readings almost always informed me in a very helpful way, sometimes startlingly so. I formed the view that it gave good answers because of the philosophic fabric of yin and yang and the Tao from which it was woven. This background would act as a mirror reflecting an aspect of reality that our Western language did not acknowledge very well. The process of using I Ching calmed my mind and I became open and receptive to the oracle. From this perspective it would not matter which reading turned up, so a random process would still deliver the goods. It sounded like a good theory, but eventually I came to think differently.

A couple of readings were so striking that I questioned whether any other one would have given me the same result. So I checked this out and determined for myself that only the reading that was actually received could answer my question with any precision. My theory was wrong! The exact reading *did* matter. How could that happen? How did the universe, as expressed through this tool, receive my questions, and then respond accurately to them? I could not control the process consciously to choose the right reading. There was something going on that my intellect could not figure out. I was determined to find out what it was.

It was a few years after that that I started to have direct experiences of the One Source expressing itself through my being and life. I came out of the atheist closet. God was expressing itself through me, through others, through everything. And it had nothing to do with my mind and my thoughts. It was not a matter of belief in some thought or idea; it was a deep knowing of an indisputable fact! Even though my personal self and my ego identifications had a sense of separateness, I knew without a doubt that this separateness was not real. The One Source was everywhere and we were connected to it by a transcendent love. We are fractal reflections of the Totality.

I wondered how I could live with this reality in everyday life. I tried a spiritual path and lived in a community devoted to surrender to this truth. Eventually, I was initiated into a meditation of surrender. I found this quite difficult. Apparently, an aspect of myself resisted surrender to the Source. Eventually, I returned to a more ordinary life on the surface, although I found that I was more distracted and less able to focus.

Then, a few years ago, a friend mentioned to me a little book, a century old, which emphasized that the key to success was a co-creative approach and an attitude of gratitude. My intuition told me that this was important. I soon determined that this co-creative approach paralleled my experiences of the One Source. But try as I might, I found it difficult to experience much gratitude, especially as an emotion. Something was missing for me.

This co-creative approach involved allowing the blossoming of our personal will and that of others, without limiting each other, and without filling our minds with thoughts of completing our will. I soon noticed an issue which had not been made explicit by anyone following this method, and that was the presence of divine will amongst all of this personal will. I became aware of the crucial role of gratitude in discerning divine will from personal ambitions. It was a question of alignment. Divine will is always present, staring us in the face, and gratitude became a kind of bridge to it. When it seemed that there was a big gap between what I personally wanted and what was actually present, gratitude actually brought these two closer together.

However, I still had difficulty feeling gratitude emotionally. Then it occurred to me that there was a subtle level of personal "doer-ship" which I had not been noticing. I had been holding the thoughts that I had to be the one to surrender, to move into alignment with Divine Will, to use my thoughts to make a better world for myself, the one to grow personally. I had got it backwards!

Then at a spiritual retreat high in the Rocky Mountains, a wonderful experience overtook me. A wish bubbled up within me to become more open to the hearts of others. In a context of complete freedom and joyful celebration with others, I started to feel the circle of all our hearts. Then something let go and my personal consciousness was on the sidelines. Only that circle, as a single heart, was present, like a necklace of jewels. I was only one aspect of that heart. Each heart was present, and yet there was only one Heart.

Several things became immediately clear to me. That One Heart is always present and is just as much what I really am as is my personal consciousness. Our consciousness is both a We and an I! This consciousness is nourished only by nourishing each of the hearts in the circle with equal respect.

This gave me a golden key for discernment. Divine will is an expression of all of our hearts, all together, not something separate which demands us to change, but something whose acceptance of each of us is total. So the key is to notice what is in the best interest of the others I am present with, and of myself. It is neither altruism, nor is it selfishness, but it includes others and personal self because it is our Greater Self.

In the months since this experience, the presence of this discernment has been growing. It shows up with my family, with my friends, with my business, in my community. It shows up whenever I am with anyone. What can deter it for me is when I allow my personal self to become too busy, to leave things to the last, to let responsibilities pile up, or when I do not look after my own body and spirit. I experience gratitude and satisfaction more easily now, and I have a lightness that comes from the knowledge that my personal self does not have to and cannot, do it all. I experience more gratitude because I have accepted that I am being nourished by the One Heart in the hearts of others, and that my personal "doing" is not what it's all about.

Now when I need to discern, I do not need some external tool like the I Ching or a horoscope or a guru. Instead, I open to the circle of hearts which I am currently with. When I am alone, I open up to a sense of the space supporting all the cells of my body, what I call "in-betweening." I feel that loving supporting space. Then I open to becoming that space and from that perspective lovingly experience the emergence of the energy and matter which make up my person. For me this is opening the heart. The same kind of in-betweening with myself and others helps me to sense the One Heart.

I have found this approach very conducive to my life as a Unitarian and a practicing Sufi. It also greatly informs my professional life, which is concerned with the dynamics of systems, organizations, economies, and how people collaborate with them. It has given a necessary focus to two books I am writing: *Return to Wholeness*, a spiritual book; and *Coherent Management*, which describes how these ideas have been applied to a successful business.

Oh yes, about the five-leaf clover patches. One day I asked through discernment what this strange and rather unique gift really meant. The answer came back strong and clear. This gift was a reminder that it was my calling in life to affirm the uniqueness of others. Then my own uniqueness would really shine forth.

Who's holier?

He also told this parable to some who trusted in themselves
that they were righteous and regarded others with contempt:
"Two men went up to the temple to pray,
one a Pharisee and the other a tax collector.
The Pharisee, standing by himself, was praying thus,
'God, I thank you that I am not like other people:
thieves, rogues, adulterers, or even like this tax collector.
I fast twice a week; I give a tenth of all my income.'
But the tax collector, standing far off,
would not even look up to heaven, but was beating his breast and saying,
'God, be merciful to me, a sinner!'
I tell you, this man went down to his home justified rather than the other;
for all who exalt themselves will be humbled,
but all who humble themselves will be exalted."
LUKE 18:9–14

Statements such as "He's so committed to God that he became a minister," or "The mystical path is the holiest," keep many people from a deep and rich relationship with the divine. Each of us is called into a unique connection and one way of being with God is only the "best" for us if that is our intended way. We have already met Yvon who was called away from ordination to use his gifts in administration.

The belief that clergy and other religious are a holier breed can keep those who don't have that call from cherishing and embracing the sacredness of their own path. This notion also contributes to a sense of isolation for many clergy. One pastor told me recently, "When my mother was dying, none of my pastoral care team at church contacted me to provide support. They do this for any other member of the congregation. I *did* receive some cards, most of which had the theme, 'I'm sure your faith is helping you through this difficult time.' Yes it is, and I also need people support."

God is passionate about relationships, about community. All are equal in the eyes of God.

Mystical experiences

Divine reality is a dazzling blend
of infinite acceptance and infinite demand.
Most people who have drunk deeply
of God have walked wildly through life.
JOHN SHEA[18]

As well as assuming people who have mystical experiences are holier, there is a widely held belief that these God-touches are rare. Furthermore, the term mystic usually refers solely to people long dead who happened to write about their experiences. Most people, at one time or another in their lives, have had a mystical experience. Some are born with a tendency to mystical experiences. This doesn't make them higher on the spiritual path. In fact, some of the most wounded people I have met in my psychotherapy practice have been those walking a mystical path.

Whatever our experience of Holy Mystery, we filter and make meaning of it through our true and false selves. Here are some statements about their gift that people who have many mystical experiences made to me.

• As a young child, I quickly realized that others did not feel the intense love and hear the inner comforting voice that I did. I hid my experience, thinking I was going crazy. I actually did become more and more off balance because I was disconnecting myself from God. I stayed away from any private or corporate worship because that really got the mystical experiences going. It wasn't until I was in my 30s that I met someone who talked about their own experiences and I started to accept my gift.

- Everyone in my church began to see me as having a direct conduit to God and would ask my advice about spiritual matters all the time. I felt I had to tell them something because they relied on me. I learned, after some unfortunate experiences where my advice really backfired, that I did not have a gift for spiritual direction.

We are all familiar with authors or other artists who produce a work that is truly inspired. Many people experience delight or healing contact with the piece. Then the artist's next work bombs. Sometimes their career is erratic – one inspiration followed by a stilted, lifeless work. We speak about the volatile artistic personality as we watch some turn to drugs, alcohol, or promiscuous sexual behavior.

My theory is that these people, consciously or unconsciously, have been deeply connected to the divine during production of their "masterpieces." If they don't realize this, an unrealistic view of their personal brilliance will close their receptivity to Spirit during production of their next work. The extreme variety in quality must be bewildering and frightening. The more the artist tries to control or force their creativity, the further away they turn from God.

Even those who have allowed God to nurture their gifts are still bound by the fact that they live in a finite body and have been influenced by family, society, and their faith tradition. Catherine of Siena, who, as we have already learned, imagined the spiritual life as a large tree, had many mystical experiences. She used these as a channel for opening people to God's love and for mediating in a number of conflicts between church authorities, bringing reconciliation and peace. She also, however, was an advocate of "holy war" and urged those same church authorities to stop fighting each other so that they would have more energy to fight in Crusades. Hearing God clearly in one area does not mean we hear clearly in all areas.

Marsha Sinetar conducted a study, which she has described in her book *Ordinary People as Monks and Mystics*. She searched out and interviewed people who were viewed in their communities as deeply spiritual. She sent out posters asking for stories from people who had regular mystical experiences. She received many. Mystics are all around us: they may, in fact, be us.

TANYA'S STORY

I think I'd like to be known as Tanya. I'm not quite ready to be completely visible in my discernment story. Since a conversion experience some years ago, I feel and see God's infinite love and desire to partner with us coloring the whole world. Initially, I felt God's presence within me as a comforting warmth.

My intent is to be receptive and oriented to this holy presence at all times. So the desire to discern is something I carry with me throughout the day. God speaks to me in many ways: through devotional reading, other people, nature, dreams, and so on.

I would have thought that experiencing God so potently would make discerning much easier. When I see creation so crammed full of divinity, though, it is sometimes more difficult to understand the path God wants me to take. My own ego certainly gets in the way. And I'm continually aware of and grateful for the gift of free will we have received.

I woke up around 3:30 a.m., a few years ago, feeling intense sexual arousal. This was very strange and disturbing because, at this time in my life, I was not feeling my sexuality very strongly. As I monitored my sensations, I wondered if I should wake my husband and do something about them. However, I felt no desire to act on this experience. I asked God within me what to do and heard/felt "Pray."

Good suggestion, I thought. That will make these sensations disappear. I was feeling rather embarrassed about this sexuality. It felt like my body was acting up to show God and me how unspiritual I really was. So I went to my "prayer chair," lit a candle and some incense, and opened more fully to God.

And found an astonishing thing. The more receptive to God I became, the stronger the sexual feelings grew. Oh no, I'm really blowing it! So I asked all the angels and saints I could think of for help. The sexual sensations just became stronger. And now I was very aware that I had a crowd of witnesses. It was extremely embarrassing.

A cold shower did not help. Thinking about something other than God *did* calm the sensations down a little, but that seemed ridiculous. To actually separate myself from God in order to appear more holy. My image of myself as a spiritual being, above all animal urges, was shattered and I was feeling miserable. That's not quite true. My emotions had a strong negative flavor. My body was zinging with life and energy.

The sexual sensations continued throughout the morning. I was afraid that other people would know and pull away from me. My husband said the sexuality wasn't visible. When he looked at me he saw an appealing vitality. I thought he was saying that to make me feel better.

That afternoon I had a spiritual direction session booked. I had very mixed feelings about going. I was so embarrassed about my sensations. And what could a celibate nun tell me about sexuality anyway? On the other hand, she must have had experience getting rid of sexual feelings, so maybe she was the best person to tell.

When Sister Jo and I met, I looked at her welcoming face and felt my own face turning red. How could I start? I said, "God is very creative." She nodded and waited. "I mean, really, really creative." She waited. "And, um, very, kind of, sexual." "Ah," she responded quite matter of factly. "Are you having experiences of making love to Jesus?" "Oh no!" I replied with horror. (Pause) "It feels like the Holy Spirit. And we're not making love. I just feel this intense sexuality and the more I open to God, the stronger it gets."

Sister Jo told me that this is an experience written about by many men and women who have mystical experiences. She suggested I open to and enjoy God in this way. Even with her support, it took me months to become easy with this aspect of Holy Mystery. The sensations were there every day. As I relaxed into the experience, I became aware of how everything in creation is being continually re-created by our loving, hands-on God.

My sensations did not urge me on to sexual activity, although I began to realize that wouldn't be wrong. They *did* encourage me to cherish creativity wherever I encountered it. And I encountered it everywhere. My director helped me to explore the sacredness of intimacy and I found my friendships deepening and broadening. At work, I became more creative; instead of viewing something or someone as a problem, I more readily saw the situation as blocked creativity and energy. How did God want this energy unblocked so that all interested parties would benefit?

I also have done a lot of changing in my beliefs about incarnation. God has given us bodies as a gift of love. We could have been created in some other form. We are to enjoy our incarnation. My body is often more truthful about a need than my mind is. I saw how I was judging my body. I thought the way to God was through my heart and mind. Books that helped me were Professor Philip Sheldrake's *Befriending our Desires* and Dr. Gerald May's *The Awakened Heart*.

Then I realized that God wanted me to use this sexual energy for discernment. I was talking to someone at work, when I felt a strong surge. "Could you please repeat what you just said," I asked. When the man reiterated his point, I could see that here was the key to our misunderstanding. And I would have missed it, but for the sexual surge.

Since then, whenever I feel that surge, I become as present as I can, to myself and to the outside world. I know God is wanting me to attend to something more fully. When I ask for direction, and hold various choices in my heart and mind, there will often be more sexual energy around one of them.

Discernment is still like an ongoing conversation, though. If a path seems to be indicated, there is work to do to clarify it and to be open to Spirit changing as circumstances change.

As I share Tanya's story in lectures, I frequently have one or more people nod with recognition and tell me later that her story matches their own experiences. Gerald May, in *The Awakened Heart*, says "Sometimes [God's Love] is felt and expressed in ways that are undeniably sexual: yearning, embracing, excitement, fulfillment, and resting so deep and physical that one can never again doubt the fullness of divine incarnation."[19]

But is Tanya holier or less holy because of her mystical experiences? If we look at her through human eyes, we will judge her based on criteria we have developed. If we try to view her as God does, we see that Tanya was invited to an experience that would shake her narrow image of herself and of her Creator. Through her "yes," Tanya grew in her ability to connect with herself, others, and God, helping her to live more as the person she is meant to be.

God loves her more; she always gets a parking space!

There is that near you that will guide you;
Oh wait for it, and be sure ye keep to it.
ISAAC PENINGTON[20]

It certainly looks like some people are more favored by God. Their lives seem to flow more smoothly. Parking spaces open before them; they're frequently in the right place at the right time. Most of us have experienced a time, whether a day or an hour, when everything seemed to fall into place. However, when we try to control our lives to ensure smooth running, the result is often an experience of rigidity and restriction, with accompanying feelings of frustration.

God does not work on a reward and punishment system. We are all loved equally and cherished for our uniqueness. The Quakers have a term "Way opens," which means moving into alignment with God's will, getting with the divine flow. When this occurs, the path naturally becomes clearer and smoother. Cultivating the qualities of receptivity and flexibilty are useful here and it may take time for way to open as shown in this next story.

BETTY MCINNES' STORY

It was the mid-1960s. The Vietnam War occupied a large place in the hearts and minds of many people throughout the world. Some were still passionately for American involvement; a growing number were passionately against. The Religious Society of Friends, often referred to as the Quakers or as The Friends, have always stood for non-violence. This has included a willingness to accept prison or other societal penalties for their beliefs.

Betty McInnes, a Friend, found that her commitment to non-violence was becoming more and more personal as her two sons neared the age where they would be drafted. Should the family leave California and move to Canada? To Betty, that felt like running away. If they stayed, they might be a good influence on others. Yet their sons would be faced with a decision about conscientious objection at too young an age.

A Quaker method of discernment, which I consciously use often, is a combination of listening for guidance and actively watching to see how the Way opens. If I am receptive, I will see where Spirit is leading me. In 1966, our family went on a holiday to visit friends at a rural Quaker community at Argenta, British Columbia, Canada. We had an enjoyable visit and learned more about the community, including their residential school for Grades 11 and 12. There was no sign, though, that Argenta would be a good place for us to settle.

In 1967, my husband, Bob, made a business trip to the Canadian province of Saskatchewan. On the way, he met with mental health care professionals in Vancouver, BC, to check out the job situation. There was nothing appropriate. The Way was not opening for us to move.

Then, in 1968, my boss suggested that we borrow his cabin on Gabriola Island, in the Canadian Gulf Islands, for our holiday. Since Gabriola is quite close to the provincial mental health office in Victoria, Bob contacted the staff there to say hello. He was offered a job!

Now we had a concrete decision to make. Was this truly Way opening? If so, there would be other signs. They came rapidly.

Our family went to the Pacific yearly meeting of the Religious Society of Friends and found the principal and teachers of the residential school in Argenta were also present. Our daughter expressed interest in attending the school and the staff were willing to interview her right then, saving us time and the expense of sending her to the school. Immediately after the interviews, we heard that they would be pleased to accept her.

Way seemed to be opening. It would be expensive, however, to pay for her tuition and board, as well as for all the relocation expenses for the rest of the family. While we were still at the yearly meeting, another Friend heard about our new plans and offered to cover some of our daughter's school costs. Another Friend asked what we were doing with our house in California and ended up buying it. With these clear signs, I was able to let go of my worry that leaving would be running away. The Way was wide open and, in gratitude, we moved.

We have probably all experienced "way opening" at some time in our lives. Some people, however, have found that they received more learning about themselves when "way closed." God is always working within us on that lemonade recipe, no matter what choices we make. And the divine does not play favorites; we are all invited to the choice that will meet our needs.

No job openings for martyrs!

[People] fear that if God's will is done, it will result in hardship,
that God's will has cutting edges and unhappy results.
They fear that God's will may be the worst thing that could happen.
Many people fear that God may require them to do almost impossible tasks.
DANNY E. MORRIS AND CHARLES M. OLSEN[21]

Actually, God *does* ask us for the hardest thing we could possibly do: to love God with our whole heart, mind, strength, and soul. And if we are loving God so totally, we will naturally love ourselves, others, and all of creation. This is a very difficult thing to do and we will spend the whole of our lives growing in our capacity for love.

Fortunately, God has given us gifts that will make our growth easier. And we can rely on God's unconditional love for us to provide support on the way. We will not be asked to "jump through hoops" to show our love. We will be called to paths that will assist us to become the people we are meant to be, with our unique gifts and circumstances.

Later in the book, we will hear about Albert Schweitzer's call to become a doctor in Africa. Over the years, Schweitzer saw many would-be martyrs who approached him for advice or approval for a path they were contemplating. He was often concerned that an unusual or dangerous path was being chosen for ego reasons: a wish for society's approval or a belief that a heavier burden demonstrated greater love of God. He suggested, "Only a person who can find a value in every sort of activity and devote himself to each one with full consciousness of duty, has the inward right to take as his object some extraordinary activity."[22]

Sometimes people approached Schweitzer complaining that they had no opportunity to be helpful in their boring lives. In talking with them, Schweitzer was often surprised by how many opportunities for service were already present in the lives of these people. They were missing opportunities for helping because they were looking for a more exciting call.

SANDRA'S STORY

For as long as I can remember, I have had a strong yearning to be connected to God, to work for God. So, as a teen, I was very active in my church and this involvement has continued in a lay, paid capacity ever since. I had lots of friends, but I remember feeling different. They didn't seem to have the passion to work for God that I did.

Throughout my growing up, there has been the strong feeling that because I have been blessed with so much, much would be asked of me. I accepted challenging ministries working with marginalized people. They were very satisfying. Yet in the back of my mind was the thought that these experiences were only a training ground for the real hard stuff that was to come.

I kept expecting God to ask something of me that I didn't want to do. When I found myself the mother of small children, I worried that God would ask our family to move somewhere that was dangerous for the kids. So I consciously stayed away from a discernment process. If I didn't ask or listen, I wouldn't know what God was wanting and I wouldn't have to consciously refuse.

I felt very guilty about this stance, but I was doing it to protect my family. I didn't think that God would realize the impact a call would have on us. Also, because of my belief that giving myself totally to God meant a hard life, I didn't ask for anything I thought would be easy or enjoyable. Whenever life became too comfortable, I felt uneasy, waiting for the other shoe to drop.

In what seemed like a separate issue, I was having difficulty in prayer really opening my heart to God. I wanted to, yet felt anxious when I tried. One day I asked God for help. In response, I saw in my mind's eye the face of a woman who I knew was on an intentional spiritual path. A voice inside me said, "Ask Marni for spiritual direction." Oh dear, this was hard. My faith tradition is not familiar with spiritual direction. And the thought of baring my soul was scary. I asked if there were another way to work on this issue and didn't get an answer.

Over the next few months, every time I asked about opening my heart, I saw Marni's face. So I finally phoned her. I said, "I'd like to see you for spiritual direction." She responded, "I don't do spiritual direction." When I explained how I was led to call her, she prayed about it and felt an encouragement from God to meet with me.

Spirit was so strongly present during our meetings. I quickly saw the connection between my difficulty trusting God with my heart and the belief that living for God meant hardship and suffering. I was stunned when Marni showed me the scripture passage, "My yoke is easy; my burden is light." Of course I had read it many times, but I had never thought it applied to me.

We met for about eight sessions. By the end of our time together, I was well on my way to trusting and opening my heart. I realized that God wanted to give abundantly to me and loved it when I asked for what I wanted. If what I thought I wanted wasn't in my best interest, by dialoguing with God about it the real need or desire became clearer. Looking back at my spiritual history, I can see how I sometimes made the path more difficult, or did not follow the openings that would have made the journey easier.

We all know and honor those people who have taken a stand for justice or freedom and have paid with their lives or health. These people were not looking to be martyrs. They were living their beliefs so fully that they they did not pull back from a risky situation when they saw it as part of their path. There are no job openings for martyrs. There are an infinite number of job openings for people who wish to partner with God to bring peace and freedom to creation.

A woman told me that one day in prayer, she said in frustration, "I'm sorry, God, I'm not able to give you all the love that I know must be inside me." The response came, "Are you giving me all you are able to right now?" "Yes," she replied. She heard, "That's enough."

Of course God wants us to help others!

There is a piece of wisdom that all the world must know;
the same Spirit who bids us to say yes also bids us to say no!
COLLEEN FULMER[23]

When we hear the call to help others, there is the tendency to see their needs as more important than our own. God wants everyone and everything in the situation to thrive. God's will for us has a broad range. Everywhere we turn, we see causes crying out for assistance. Some people become so overwhelmed by the number of worthy causes that they close down and numb themselves as protection. "What could an individual like me possibly do that would make a difference?" they say.

It's always win-win with God. Our path will help ourselves and others as we are called to use our gifts. For example, if I discern a call to promote justice in my world, I could obtain further education and work in the court system or prisons; I could join a citizens' group supporting survivors of crime; I could offer programs at my child's elementary school to help discourage bullying; I could learn communication skills, such as Dr. Marshall Rosenberg's Non-violent Communication, so that my family, friends, and co-workers experience me as living in a just manner.

By being receptive to a process of discernment, I can determine which, if any, of these activities God would have me do.

ALIDA'S STORY

I had not thought to ask God what to do in a situation that seemed so clear. I was walking slowly, enjoying the sights, sounds, and smells of the city. I had a free afternoon, my husband was picking up the kids from school, and I had decided to spend it people watching and window shopping. The snow was almost completely gone; this was the first bootless day for me. The delightful feeling of physical freedom was tempered by the need to watch my footing. The long winter had been rough on the streets and sidewalks. Cracks and holes could mean a sprained or broken ankle.

Ahead of me, an elderly woman was returning home from her shopping expedition with her wheeled cart piled high. Just as I focused my attention on her, one of the cart wheels caught a large crack in the pavement and the cart twisted out of her hands and fell sideways. Groceries scattered. Here was a situation that called for assistance.

During my walk, I had been quite receptive to God, giving thanks for the spring day and having the sense that we were enjoying the world together. So as I started forward to offer my help, I said in the depths of my heart, "One of your children is in need, I'll be your hands." The response I got brought me up short!

I usually know God's will for me by a deep feeling of rightness and peace. I didn't have that feeling now! In fact, there was more of a feeling of a breath being held. I stood, confused and flustered. How could God not want me to help this woman? She had just got her cart righted and here I was doing nothing but watching. Yet I wasn't getting that inner confirmation that God wanted me to act.

I noticed two adolescent boys leaning against the front window of a small store. The accident was momentarily more interesting than the game of hacky-sack they had been playing. As I looked at them, the older one's gaze left the woman for a moment to glance at me. Now embarrassment was added to my confusion. I thought he had looked at me with judgment. My face flamed red.

Only a few moments had elapsed; the woman had just begun to pick up her spilled belongings. "Where are you, God? What am I to do!" I thought silently but forcefully. At that moment, the older teen pushed away from the wall, walked over to the accident scene, and started placing groceries carefully in the cart. I heard him say to the woman, "I work part-time in a grocery. You got to put the heavy stuff in first or it will crush the other things." They worked side by side in silence for a few minutes. I glanced at the younger teen, who had an expression of surprise on his face. An expression which was mirrored on mine.

Work completed, the woman spoke her thanks, gave her helper a radiant smile, and walked on. As the boy rejoined his friend, I heard the younger one ask, "What did you do that for?" "Don't know," was the response. "Just felt like it."

I continued on my walk with my mind and heart full of gratitude and questions. If I had helped, would he have? Was that the first time he had thought to assist another not of his group? I wonder how God spoke to him? I prayed that he would continue to be receptive to God's voice.

There were also prejudices and assumptions I needed to examine. In similar situations, I have felt that if I didn't help, no one would. What a judgmental attitude. Here I am, God's little helper. Indispensable! And I don't expect others to listen to God. I don't expect God to be able to get through to them. I assume that my idea of helping is the best one. I prayed that I also would be receptive to God's voice.

That afternoon was a real turning point for me. Since then, I am more aware of how only God has the big picture. I try to watch my assumptions and realize how active the Holy Spirit is in everyone and everything. Our God is a God of relationships. I am called to specific tasks. Just because I see a need does not mean that I am the one to meet it. I had not thought to ask God what to do in a situation that seemed so clear.

When we are touched by the Holy who gives to us so lavishly, there can be a strong urge to give back as lavishly as we can. Peace Pilgrim says that early in her spiritual path, "I was filled with a runaway enthusiasm to help others, and one could argue that when I solved so many problems for others I was depriving them of the spiritual growth problem-solving brings. I soon realized I had to leave some good works for others to do and be blessed by."[24]

People come to me frequently and say, "I feel led by God to see you for psychotherapy." I always check within myself to determine if I am being told directly or indirectly that this is also divine will for me. The other person may be hearing clearly. Or they may have clarified the message partially.

They may have come to the awareness that psychotherapy would be beneficial in their life right now and I am the only psychotherapist they know, so they approach me. Or, they are being led to ask me about psychotherapy and I am to suggest the appropriate agency or person for them. There can be many reasons they have come to me. By taking their request, made in God's name, literally, I may be doing both of us a disservice.

Pray always, discern always

Rejoice always, pray without ceasing,
give thanks in all circumstances.
1 Thessalonians 5:16–18a

"Impossible!" you say. "Exhausting even if it were possible!" Actually, praying and discerning without ceasing involves more of an attitude shift than a behavioral one. As Patricia Loring explains, "this does not mean continually saying prayers. Rather it is bringing into our outward lives the openness of consciousness and heart that we practice in private."[25]

When a beloved friend comes to visit, we orient to that person: mind, heart, body, and soul. Even if we are in another room or have to go to the store for a forgotten item, we never forget that our friend is in our home. The presence of our friend with us is gentle on our mind. We do not need to strain to keep our attention there.

God doesn't have to be invited to visit. Although the Source of our Being is already living with us, because we have free will, our consent is needed for the Presence to be made visible. And we do need God's assistance; for this type of intimacy is like learning to dance together. It takes time and practice. Unceasing prayer and discernment are connected. Patricia Loring views discernment as a dimension or concomitant of unceasing prayer.

The following story describes a particular method for developing unceasing prayer that comes from the Russian Orthodox tradition.

A RUSSIAN SERF'S STORY

In *The Way of a Pilgrim*, R. M. French relates that the seeker left his journal at the Russian Orthodox monastery at Mount Athos. He did not sign it. We know from his writing that he was a serf in the mid-1800s. Due to a fall when he was seven years old, he couldn't use his left arm. This greatly limited the work he could do, although he was taught to write by a frequent traveler to his grandfather's inn. As an adult, after suffering losses through arson, and later through the death of the wife he dearly loved, he decided on the life of a pilgrim.

Since he was unable to work due to his crippled arm, our serf was able to procure a passport which allowed him to travel unhindered. With his Bible in his knapsack, he began his pilgrimage, initially with no direction in mind. Shortly after, he experienced an urge to travel to holy sites and ask for help in his troubles. His pilgrimage for healing lasted many years. The following story, in his words, is taken from Helen Bacovcin's translation of *The Way of a Pilgrim*. The honesty and clarity with which the seeker tells the tale of his spiritual ups and downs makes for interesting reading.

On the 24th Sunday after Pentecost I came to church to attend the Liturgy and entered just as the epistle was being read. The reading was from Paul's First Letter to the Thessalonians, which says in part, "Pray constantly." These words made a deep impression on me and I started thinking of how it could be possible for a man to pray without ceasing when the practical necessities of life demand so much attention...I thought and thought about these words, but no understanding came to me."[26]

Our pilgrim could not get the puzzle out of his mind and heart. He began to travel with even more purpose, looking for someone who could show him how to pray without ceasing. Every wise person he encountered talked with him about prayer. No one could teach him to do it.

After journeying for a time, he was overtaken on the road one evening by an old man, who from his manner and dress looked like a monk. In response to the old man's questioning, the pilgrim related the story of his quest. The monk invited him to come to his monastery which was about ten versts (approximately seven miles) up the road. Our pilgrim responded, "My peace does not depend on a place to stay but on spiritual direction. I am not looking for food as I have enough bread in my knapsack." (Bacovcin, p. 15–16)

The monk was very interested in these statements and inquired as to the type of spiritual direction he was seeking. Once he understood,

> the elder blessed himself and began to speak: "Thank God, dear brother, for this insatiable desire to understand ceaseless mental prayer. Recognize this as a call from God and be at peace. Believe that up to this time your seeking was in accordance with God's will and you were given to understand that heavenly light regarding continuous prayer is not reached by worldly wisdom and superficial curiosity." (Bacovcin, p. 16)

The monk offered to become his starets and teach our pilgrim the way of unceasing prayer. He taught the pilgrim to use the Jesus prayer, "Lord Jesus Christ, have mercy on me," as a mantra. As instructed, our pilgrim repeated it with increasing frequency. At first, his whole mind was taken up with this prayer. In time, he felt as if it were praying him, and was able to do other activities simultaneously.

As we have just seen, some people feel called to specific practices for developing unceasing prayer. For others, the desire to be consciously aware of and present to God at all times is enough to start the process of unceasing prayer and discernment. Sometimes, in fact, the practice of mindfullness, being as present as possible, is the path.

How do I know it's God?

God's will is found in doing what we want at the very best and
deepest level of who we understand ourselves to be.
KATHERINE DYCKMAN AND PATRICK CARROLL[27]

A discernment process involves God's longing to be visible to us, rather than deciding on a course of action based solely on what would enhance our status in society, give us more money, or keep us safer. So it is important to separate, to the best of our ability, God's voice from the voices of our false self, society, other people or forces. As Patricia Loring says, "We may mistake our thoughts or agendas for the movement of the Spirit, or we may become so involved in them that we are oblivious to the motions of the Spirit."[28]

Sometimes the guidance is so clear that no further discernment is necessary. Even then, as D. V. Steere puts it, "Few concerns reveal more than an inkling of all that they contain, and those that carry them out must always expect to be vulnerable."[29] If your message is not clear, the following points may help. They have been drawn from my interviews and from a number of spiritual guides.

1. "God never guides us to break divine law and if such a negative guidance comes to us we can be sure it is not from God." [30]

2. "A basic method is to note the final result. Does it lead to humility or to pride, to looking beyond ourselves or into ourselves?"[31] Another way of expressing this is to look at the "fruits" of the leading.

3. What effect does the choice have on our spirituality, on how we live life's meaning? God always calls us towards communion, with God and with others. Some feel a closer connection with the divine in solitary spiritual practices. This experience gives them the nurturing, rest, and guidance they need to then reach out in service. Even hermits and other contemplatives have a call to service, usually in many hours of intercessory prayer. So if you seem called to escape from the world, you need to examine that call closely.

4. What are the people who are connected with this discernment saying? What's their response? If they do not agree with our choice, they may be hearing something from God that we are not. Or their own egos might be distorting their message. It is worth spending some time checking our discernment with others.

5. Since we are all strands on the vast web of creation, we need to be aware of the environmental and cultural impact/influences of our choice.

6. God does not subscribe to the adage, "If you snooze, you lose." We will receive more than one message. Often, being receptive over time allows us to refine the guidance. Louis Savary S.J. suggests taking one option and living the next week as though this were the one you have chosen. Watch for divine support for this option through things people say who don't know you are in a discernment process, and through books and music that jump out at you, etc. Then, at the end of the week, take the option to worship and offer it and yourself to God. Be aware of the feeling you have after doing this. Are you peaceful, feeling balanced or quietly determined? Or agitated, excited? Then take the second option and live with it for a week. Take it to worship. By this time it may become clear to you which option to accept. If not, wait for further guidance or try another method if you feel called to it.

7. Do you have a sense of detachment about the options? Detachment does not mean disinterest or unresponsiveness. It *does* imply a surrender to the longing of God, knowing that by doing so your own deepest needs and desires will be met. "We are free interiorly with the experience that we think may be a call." (English, p. 181) If we have a vested interest in one option, it will be very difficult to determine on our own what God is telling us. It is then most helpful to ask others for help. There are a number of stories in later sections which speak to this issue.

8. "Discernment moves you to holy ground, the arena of divine presence and will. Holy ground may not be familiar territory."[32] So often we assume that a sense of discomfort means something is not good. Ignatian spirituality suggests looking instead at whether the message brings consolation or desolation. Consolation can be described as "comfort, peace and quiet, calmness, and union with God." (English, p. 127) Desolation, on the other hand, is an experience of painful disconnection from God. It can be important to stay with a feeling of desolation for a while and explore it. It may mean this option is not the one for us. It may also mean that we need to allow some transformation within ourselves before it is appropriate to act on this message.

9. Judging God's will based on whether or not the call will mean a change in direction for us needs to be done carefully. Examining the meaning of the message in terms of the awarenesses we have had over the last while – types of personal growth we have recently experienced, past leadings from God – and then looking at the new direction within this context, may help.

10. Does the message pull you away from spiritual practice? If you find yourself too busy with the new project to take time to "drink at the well," there is a problem with your listening.

11. "Among Friends the spiritual fruit, patience, was perhaps the central test of moral purity. With good reason, promptings serving primarily the individual's own will or ego-needs…are more apt to be pressing, impatient of restraint and evanescent. Promptings truly of divine origin are more likely to persist over time, despite outward checks."[33]

12. Does the message lead to true freedom or illusionary freedom? We have all experienced a sense of anxiety and pressure when an important decision needs to be made, and the subsequent relief when an option is chosen, even if we do not really agree with it. It feels enough not to have to think about it anymore. Ambiguity can be very uncomfortable. Making a decision to "get it off our back" is one type of the illusionary freedom of self-indulgence. "Self-indulgence – far from freedom – usually involves permitting ourselves to be overmastered, controlled or even compelled by our desires or other passing emotions."[34]

ALBERT SCHWEITZER'S STORY

Albert Schweitzer had not planned to become a doctor, much less one who would work in Equatorial Africa. He was already known as a brilliant theologian, philosopher, organist and musicologist, and certainly had enough demands on his time to keep him fully occupied with meaningful activity.

Social service had always been of great interest to him, however. As a student, he was part of a group that visited and provided financial assistance to a number of poor families every week. Due to this experience, he came to the realization that working alone was not an effective way to help the poor.

> I was resolved to put my services at the disposal of some organization, if it should be really necessary, I nevertheless never gave up the hope of finding a sphere of activity to which I could devote myself as an individual and as wholly free. That this longing of mine found fulfillment I have always regarded as a signal instance of the mercy which has again and again been vouchsafed to me.[35]

At this time, Schweitzer was principal of the Theological College of St. Thomas. A woman friend was in the habit of leaving copies of the Paris Missionary Society's newsletter on Schweitzer's writing table in the college. It was an autumn evening in 1904 and Schweitzer saw the familiar green-colored magazine. He was about to put it aside, but "mechanically opened" it instead. His eye was caught by the title of an article: "The needs of the Congo Mission." He read that the mission was in desperate need of "men and women who can reply simply to the Master's call, 'Lord I am coming'." After finishing the article, he quietly returned to his work, knowing his search was over.

Schweitzer was 29 at this time. He felt God was telling him he was needed as a physician in the Congo. This would mean years of medical school to receive the appropriate preparation and degree. "I wanted to be a doctor that I might be able to work without having to talk." (Schweitzer, p. 77) Schweitzer had enjoyed his role as preacher and professor; now he felt that his call was to *practice* the religion of love rather than just talk about it.

His discernment was distinctly unpopular. "My relatives and my friends all joined in expostulating with me on the folly of my enterprise." (Schweitzer, p. 73) They told him he was "burying the talent entrusted to me, leaving gifts and acquirement in science and art unused, being like a general who wanted to go into the firing line." (Schweitzer, p. 73) They said that lecturing about conditions in the Congo would do more good than actually going there. They guessed at his motive for going: disappointment at the slow growth of his reputation, precociousness, unfortunate love relations.

To ease his own mind that God really had called him to this path, Schweitzer thoroughly explored the call, including his physical, mental, emotional and spiritual gifts, and any challenges that were applicable. " I was conscious that every start upon an untrodden path is a venture which only in unusual circumstances looks sensible and likely to be successful." (Schweitzer, p. 75)

IGNATIUS OF LOYOLA'S STORY

Ignatius was filled with romantic chivalry when, as a Basque warrior, he went to war against the French. Then a musket ball badly shattered his leg and Ignatius was taken for convalescence to his brother's castle of Loyola. The first excruciating operation did not leave the leg with an appearance attractive enough for him, so Ignatius underwent a second.

During the long recovery, Ignatius was extremely bored. Always a man of action, with a fiery temper, the life of an invalid was trying. To help himself tolerate his enforced inactivity, Ignatius spent many hours with a vivid daydream of himself as chivalrous knight, engaging in great deeds and winning the favor of a princess.

He also had access to two books: one on the life of Christ, and the other a small book on the Christian saints. Since there was nothing else to read, Ignatius spent much time with them. Soon a second daydream was added. For hours, he imagined following Christ, not only imitating the saints, but outdoing them in the hardships he would endure for his leader.

The two daydreams gave him much enjoyment. Over time, he realized that the afterglow of these daydreams was different. "When he finished the dreams of doing the great deeds of chivalry, he felt sad and out of sorts; but when he finished the dreams of following Christ and imitating the saints, he continued to feel joyous and content."[36] His conclusion: the good spirit, God, inspired the Christ daydreams, the bad spirit inspired the daydreams that fed his ego.

God had called Ignatius of Loyola to an intentional spiritual path. Ignatius' "yes" ultimately resulted in the Society of Jesus: the Jesuits. In an attempt to assist people on their own spiritual path, Ignatius produced, among other works, *The Spiritual Exercises*.

"How do I know it's God?" asks this section heading. Even with all the suggestions in this book there are times when you may not be certain. At these points, make the decision that seems best to you. And remember that God does not leave in disgust when we make a mistake. If we are receptive, mistakes make great learning experiences.

Threat to "Yes" – The problem of evil

The battle to heal human evil always begins at home.
And self-purification will always be our greatest weapon.
M. Scott Peck[37]

Religions range widely in whether they believe evil exists and, if they believe it does, in how they believe evil manifests in the world. Regardless of their religion, many people have experienced a feeling of sick despair that seems to go beyond regular "bad vibes," whenever they are in contact with a particular person or place. Or they might wonder if an inner urge to act in life-restricting ways reflects their own ego built patterns or comes from some inimical force.

If evil *does* appear to be a factor in your life, do not try to deal with it alone. Regardless of your belief about its cause, an intelligent supernatural being or the energy generated by human acts of cruelty, it is too large and has existed too long for one person to handle.

Immediately call for God's assistance and protection. Verbalize your commitment to living aligned with the Holy. Distance yourself as soon as possible and in all ways from the experience of evil. If you are still concerned, the various religions have people who are trained to deal with evil.

Given all of the above, most of our negative or disturbing experiences are due to patterns of human attitudes and behavior.

ST. TERESA OF AVILA'S STORY

Teresa of Avila, reformer of the Carmelite order in the 16th century, is one of the most widely known Christian mystics. She has written a number of books that speak about varieties of prayer and spiritual experience. This story is from her autobiography, *The Life of St. Teresa of Jesus*. Teresa described a frequent vision she had of Jesus Christ.

Many reproaches and many vexations have I borne while telling [people about my vision] – many suspicions and much persecution also. So certain were they to whom I spoke that I had an evil spirit, that some would have me exorcised. I did not care much for this; but I felt it bitterly when I saw that my confessors were afraid to hear me...

Notwithstanding all this, I never could be sorry that I had had these heavenly visions; nor would I exchange even one of them for all the wealth and all the pleasures of the world...I used to go to [Jesus] to complain of all these hardships; and I came away from prayer consoled, and with renewed strength. I did not dare to contradict those who were trying me; for I saw that it made matters worse, because they looked on my doing so as a failure in humility...

As my visions grew in frequency, one of those who used to help me before...began to say that I was certainly under the influence of Satan. He bade me, now that I had no power of resisting, always to make the sign of the cross when I had a vision, to point my finger at it by way of scorn, and be firmly persuaded of its diabolical nature. If I did this, the vision would not recur…This was a great hardship for me, for as I could not believe that the vision did not come from God, it was a fearful thing for me to do; and I could not wish, as I said before, that the visions should be withheld.

However, I did at last what I was bidden. I prayed much to our Lord that He would deliver me from delusions…It was to me a most painful thing to make a show of contempt whenever I saw our Lord in a vision: for when I saw Him before me, if I were to be cut in pieces, I could not believe it was Satan. This was to me, therefore, a heavy kind of penance; and accordingly, that I might not be so continually crossing myself, I used to hold a crucifix in my hand. This I did almost always…

[Jesus] said to me that I was not to distress myself – that I did well to obey; but He would make them see the truth of the matter. He seemed to me to be angry when they made me give up my prayer. He told me to say to them that this was tyranny. He gave me reasons for believing that the vision was not satanic [a strong increase in her love for God and her desire to deepen this relationship].[38]

TOM'S STORY

I had been on an intentional spiritual path for a few years when I had an experience of evil. At first, I didn't know what was happening to me. I was a board member for a non-profit society and had just left our monthly meeting. They are situated in an old house on a quiet residential street. It was just after 8 p.m., dark, and looking like rain. I couldn't hear any traffic and so, stepped out between two parked cars, in order to cross the street to my van. I heard brakes squeal and a car stopped two feet away from me. I was startled and so was he. The driver made an obscene gesture with his finger and yelled an expletive. This kind of thing happens periodically.

What happened next was not usual. A voice inside me, that sounded like mine, said, "Curse him back. You have the power. Make him pay." Now, I do get angry and I was definitely off balance with the near accident and the fellow's hostile reaction. The most extreme response I would be likely to make would be to say something like, "Don't drive so fast," in an angry tone. This voice, though, was encouraging violence. I made myself smile at the driver and say, "Sorry." He looked startled for a moment, put his finger down, and smiled back. We waved at each other and I continued across the street.

To go home, I traveled the freeway. About 20 minutes later, a car from the fast lane cut in front of me, causing me to brake to avoid a collision. Immediately, I heard the same voice, "Curse her, it's easy. A spiritual person's curses have more power. They'll know to keep out of your way. You'll be safer. She's upset you, make her pay." The accompanying sensation was a strong exhilaration.

I felt fear. As soon as possible, I exited the highway and stopped by the side of the road. There was a feeling of uncleanness in the car. I had a headache. I crossed myself a number of times and repeated. "I am God's. I reject all evil. God, help me. Evil depart from me. Jesus, protect me." After a few minutes, the unclean sensation was gone, the headache was gone, and I was left shaking.

In thinking later about the experience, it seemed that evil had chosen such an inconsequential situation. I wasn't an important spiritual light in the world. I wasn't being encouraged to actually kill someone. I was not being offered my greatest desire in return for my soul. Yet, as I pondered the experience, I saw that giving in to the voice and enjoying the power of putting someone else down would make that path of self-centeredness easier.

There have been similar experiences a few more times and I imagine they will continue. I talked to a spiritual guide about them and related how scared I felt. She told me that evil cannot harm me without my permission. I had done the right thing, calling for help, rejecting evil, aligning myself with God. Now I can open to protection without feeling afraid.

I find it interesting how the experience of evil so often encourages me to turn up the volume of desire or emotion I'm already feeling. Like being irritated and hearing, "Curse him," or wanting a piece of pie and hearing, "If you wait until your friend is gone, you can have the whole thing." But there is definitely a difference for me between my own selfishness and irritability, and the experience of evil. It's hard to describe – feeling unclean and excited is the closest I can come to it.

Some people have experiences similar to Tom's. More often the wrongness we encounter in life comes from our own acts and some people believe they can never be forgiven. They view themselves through the eyes of ego rather than through the divine eyes of compassion and love. The Source of Our Being hopes that we will not use our free will to hold on to our past wrongdoings. For if we regret an action or lack of action, we are already turning towards God.

Discerning through restrictions

Healer of our every ill, light of each tomorrow,
give us peace beyond our fear, and hope beyond our sorrow.
In the pain and joy beholding, how your grace is still unfolding.
Give us all your vision, God of love.
MARTY HAUGEN [39]

All people are precious and valued. God takes our restrictions and life changes into consideration. Whether through illness, traumatic accident, or a deteriorating condition such as Alzheimer's disease or MS, the divine will not only adjust our path, but will adjust the mode of communication.

ADELE'S STORY

Three years ago, Adele was driving on a mountain road, when an impaired driver smashed into her car. Unconscious for some time, Adele remembers nothing of the accident or of the surgeries that saved her life. Broken neck, mangled leg, damaged face – all had to be worked on. If the accident had occurred only a few years earlier, the microscopic surgery that was used on her extensively would not have been available and Adele would have died.

Today, Adele still has surgery to anticipate. The operations have to be spaced so she has time to recover her strength between each. Through the long, painful rehabilitation process, Adele says her faith has kept her going. She is adjusting to the realities of her life. She will never live pain free. She will be limited in her walking. The effects of her head injury include extreme fatigue, concentration problems, difficulty thinking abstractly, short-term memory loss, and slower thinking and understanding.

Knowing she is a woman of deep faith, I asked Adele how she knows what God wants her to do. This is her response.

I was so involved with my community before the accident. I frequently sang solo in my church and was in the choir. I chose the United Church of Canada when I was 14 and became deeply involved as a member, participating and volunteering in many ways. I took leading parts in community theater productions. Hairdressing was a passion of mine and I worked full time. I still had energy to spend time with my children, grandchildren, and dogs. Life was so full.

Now it is full of medical appointments and reminders to have naps so I can do whatever has to be done to survive. I certainly went through many ups and downs during this healing, sometimes being angry at God, myself, my friends, family, and the medical people.

Before the accident, if I wasn't sure whether the Lord wanted me to go with "A" or "B," I would hold each in my mind and wait to see which was accompanied by a feeling of deep peace and "rightness." That's the one I'd go with. Now I can't do that. With my head injury, I can't keep the thought in my mind long enough to get an answer. I often forget what the question is.

For a long time after the accident, I knew my focus needed to be on healing and rehabilitation. Recently, though, I have felt a little more energy and wondered how I would know God's will, since the old discernment way did not work. One day, to help me remember, I held out my hands, palm up, and said, "Lord, 'A' is in my right hand and 'B' is in my left. Which do you want me to do?" And you know what? One hand heated up! It is so clear which way to go. I do that frequently now. Sometimes the answer comes immediately and sometimes I have to wait for a while. For me, now, it has to be clear and concrete.

People who are used to communicating with God in a certain way and then deteriorate so they cannot use this method, may frustrate themselves and feel alienated from or abandoned by the Creator by trying longer and harder to force the old way to work. Caring others may be able to help the suffering person look to see how the divine is speaking to them.

ANNE'S STORY

Anne died at 103 years of age and I only knew her in the last months of her life. In that short time, her story and presence touched me deeply. In her later years, Anne was bedridden – this woman who had been a very active and gifted teacher all her adult life. Although she reminded God frequently that she was ready to die, Anne also asked to live the divine's will for her fully to the end.

Anne found comfort and connection in prayer, and did a lot of it. She soon noticed that others – friends, family, nursing staff, and strangers – seemed to want to be in her room to pray with her, to tell her their problems and pains, and to talk about God. So she said "yes" to this new ministry. She took a young immigrant woman under her wing and taught her English. She worked actively with God to fashion a ministry that met her unique situation and that used her wonderful talents.

ERIC'S STORY

When 89-year-old Eric heard I was writing this book, his eyes lit up and he said, "I'd like to tell you about my angels." I met with him and his 62-year-old son, Bob. Since Eric has had a number of large and small strokes over the past 10 years, he sometimes has difficulty matching his thoughts to his words. Bob helped with the translation. "I always felt I was doing God's work in the world. I followed the scriptures and lived giving what I had to other people," Eric stated.

Bob continued:

> Dad tried to reflect God's love. He was very active in the world. He had been a Scout leader for many years. He won community awards for his garden; he canned enough fruit and vegetables each year to feed his family and friends; and he swam in the Seniors' Games well into his 80s.
>
> Then the strokes became more frequent and he had to let go of many activities. Dad did not take this loss easily. (Eric nodded.) He became severely depressed and frequently spoke of suicide. Medication and counseling helped some of the symptoms, but he still grieved the apparent meaninglessness of his life. I was so worried for him and nothing we said made him feel better. In fact, taking him to church just got him talking about how he couldn't sing in the choir anymore because he couldn't read the words correctly. Also, he fell asleep frequently in church. So Dad worried that he was not able to do God's will anymore and talked about envying people who were still "productive."
>
> About a year ago, I noticed an increasing serenity in Dad; while we were together, Dad often just sat beaming at everyone. He rarely talked about depression. The staff at the nursing home frequently commented on his new happiness. When I asked him about his new mood, Dad said it was because of his angels. This was the first time I had ever heard him talk about this. His connection to God had always been through the scriptures.

Eric took up the story and over a half-hour period was able to tell me the following.

My angels help me... I ask them questions and they answer inside my head in my voice but I know it's them because the answers are so loving... They are always telling me that they love me... They help me feel better about myself by loving me and I know God loves me... I know it's more than one angel and they speak in a unitive voice... I feel happy that I know they're there.

Eric now knows that he is following the Holy One's plan for him by living in a receptive way. Although he feels frustration and sorrow at times, as further physical and mental deterioration is experienced, he more often is at peace and in active relationship with his angels.

As well as discovering that our Creator is with us through the pain and restriction of life, many find that they grow closer to God during times of hardship. As Albert Camus states so vividly, "In the depths of winter, I finally learned that within me there lay an invincible summer."

Qualities for effective discernment

Let us use the different gifts allotted to each of us by God's grace.
ROMANS 12:6

We have been made in the image of God and by cultivating the gifts we have been given we develop a deeper intentional relationship with the divine. The qualities of God are many. As I read over all the stories in this book, the realization came that a few qualities were present in most of them. Some of my storytellers even emphasized these qualities as essential for effective discernment. They include receptivity, patience, trust, and a willingness to participate actively. A fifth quality, love, was frequently mentioned as within and supporting the others. The following stories specifically illustrate each quality.

Receptivity

When the muse comes to dine, you have to be at home.
DOUGLAS V. STEERE[40]

Receptivity is a stance of being open to accepting the idea of the new, the unknown and many storytellers said this quality was essential for moving them past restrictions in thought and feeling. Yet receptivity also implies being open to staying the same, when that is called for. As the poet relates in Ecclesiastes 3:1, "For everything there is a season, and a time for every matter under heaven."

LAMA MARGARET'S STORY

I have been a Buddhist nun for 24 years. Our tradition emphasizes taking direction from our teachings. To discern clearly, faith, correct motivation, and correct attitude are necessary. People come to me, as a spiritual mentor, wanting me to make their decision for them. I help them clarify their goals and then assist them to change the negative energy within their attitudes and actions to positive energy. Then they will more naturally choose the best option. Once the stream has been cleared of obstacles, the water will flow more freely.

I conduct regular weekly education meetings, workshops, and retreats to help people connect with the divine within us, the Creative Force, the All-Mind. Spiritual practices help us to become open to the divine energy as we empty ourselves of ego.

Recently I was asked to give a talk to a group I didn't know. I wanted to speak the right words, yet I felt that taking a lot of time for preparation would make the talk stilted. I wanted to be receptive to the needs I perceived from the group and to where the divine energy within wanted me to go.

I first invoked the divine within me, saying, "May the right words come. May I make the right decision." Then I trusted that this would happen. During the talk I stayed as present as I could be, receptive to the energies from within and around me. After my talk, I gave thanks, expressing my deep gratitude to be connected with the divine in this way.

Receptivity without love tends to be limited to what ego decides to allow. Cultivating receptivity with love will exercise our "listening" muscle, helping us to hear the divine more clearly.

Patience

Some people will never learn anything because they grasp too soon.
Wisdom, after all, is not a station you arrive at,
but a manner of traveling...
To know exactly where you're headed may be the best way to go astray.
Not all who loiter are lost.
ANTHONY DE MELLO[41]

The realization that God is in the process of our life can help us to value the journey as well as the destination. Walking life's path with love for self, others, creation, and our Sustainer keeps patience from turning into a martyred enduring.

MARY BAKER EDDY'S STORY

The founder of Christian Science – the term she introduced to describe "the scientific system of divine healing" – made her discovery in 1866, after a long search. Mary Baker Eddy said that, "God had been graciously preparing me during many years for the reception of this final revelation of the absolute divine Principle of scientific mental healing."[42]

When the revelation came that "...Mind is All-in-all, that the only realities are the divine Mind and idea" (Eddy, p. 109), Mary was "...near the confines of mortal existence, standing already within the shadow of the death-valley..." (Eddy p. 108), after enduring many years of ill-health. Once she had the Principle, Mary looked for the way to put it into practice.

"For three years after my discovery, I sought the solution of this problem of Mind-healing, searched the Scriptures and read little else, kept aloof from society, and devoted time and energies to discovering a positive rule." (Eddy, p. 109) With her ill-health, Mary could be excused for searching frantically for the goal. Although she was one-pointed in her search, she cultivated the quality of patience.

This enabled her path to be

> sweet, calm, and buoyant with hope, not selfish or depressing. I knew the Principle of all harmonious Mind-action to be God, and that cures were produced in primitive Christian healing by holy, uplifting faith; but I must know the Science of this healing, and I won my way to absolute conclusions through divine revelation, reason, and demonstration. (Eddy, p. 109)

Sue Monk Kidd uses many analogies to describe patience, including being in a cocoon and being bread dough. Of the latter she says, "To create newness you have to cover the soul and let grace rise. You must come to the place where there's nothing to do but brood, as God brooded over the deep, and pray and be still and trust that the holiness that ferments the galaxies is working in you too. Only wait."[43]

Trust

You who dwell in the shelter of our God, who abide in this shadow for life,
say to the Lord: "My refuge, my Rock in whom I trust!"
"And I will raise you up on eagle's wings, bear you on the breath of dawn,
make you to shine like the sun, and hold you in the palm of my hand."
MICHAEL JONCAS [44]
PSALM 91

If I am deeply trusting, I have the confidence that God will be with me through thick or thin and be closer to me than my breath. This story shows how, through trust, over time, the path was found.

NORM'S STORY

Just over a year ago, Reverend Norm Tauber and his wife, Renate, realized that it was time to move on. Although they loved their ministry at Emmanuel Baptist Church, the Spirit was urging them to something new. They just didn't know what it was. Over the year they put out feelers for other churches who were looking for a ministry team in the areas of youth and young adults. They had been doing this type of ministry for 21 years and still found it immensely satisfying.

Some churches approached them, others they applied to, but in most cases the "fit" just wasn't there. A few positions seemed tailor-made, yet at the last minute the job fell through. Norm and Renate talked about the roadblocks and decided to stop looking. They felt certain that God wanted them to do something, but they weren't sure where this would be. They trusted that God would find a way to show them the right path.

A few months later, as Norm tells it, "Out of the blue, I received a phone call. 'How would you like to come to Olds, Alberta?' I said, 'Where's Olds, Alberta?' and heard laughter. I realized I was on speaker phone." The committee told him that they knew he had been looking for a new position, they had checked him out with people who knew him well, and they had prayed.

Then the surprise came. "We don't want you as youth pastor, though. We already have one we are happy with. We want you to do everything you do now, but with adults." If this was where God was wanting Norm, no wonder he hadn't found it on his own. Norm and Renate would never have thought of applying for a ministry with adults. They had always worked with youth and had assumed they would continue with that ministry. Also, Norm was used to big cities and hadn't thought to check out smaller communities.

When Norm reminded the committee of his work history, they responded, "Well, you are getting older." Norm and Renate talked together, then discussed the position with friends. During two more conference telephone calls, Norm realized that he experienced an increasing sense of peace as he contemplated this new ministry.

Then, Norm and Renate traveled to Olds and over a weekend met with every committee in the church. Although the meetings went well, they both felt disturbed. "Something was bugging me; something was wrong." Did God not want them to take this ministry?

As they clarified their feelings, the couple realized that they were deeply sad for their friends at Emmanuel Baptist, who didn't know this job was being considered. They thought of the grieving associated with leaving their ministry, their community, their home. If this feeling that something was wrong was only reluctance to make the transition, then Norm and Renate would say "yes" to God, allow the grieving, and take the new job. They wanted to be sure, however, that this was God's will.

> The First Baptist committee told me that the congregation was taking a vote about whether to offer us the ministry. The committee members would accept 75 percent in favor. That wasn't enough for us, though. I prayed that God would make it really clear for us. Either we would fail greatly or the vote would be so high there would be no doubt. The vote was 98 percent in favor of us.

This was a clear message, yet they were still feeling torn from both sides.

Norm and Renate left the decision until the last minute so they could monitor their emotions. It became clear to them that the reluctance they experienced was grief. They had a challenge ahead of them to deal openly with the issues and feelings that they and members of their current congregation would experience. They trusted that as the transition was made consciously and slowly, an increasing sense of peace would be present. They said "yes." Two weeks after telling the people at Emmanuel Baptist, Norm and Renate began to feel the peace again.

Complete trust does not mean blind trust. Norm and Renate trusted that God would show them the path to take and used the minds God had given them to question and explore different ways. They could trust because they knew they were being guided by a loving God. Trust without love tends to be rigid and blind.

Active participation

Utter dependence on God must be balanced by courageous initiative.
Each of us has a double relationship
and is required to develop a double correspondence.
EVELYN UNDERHILL[45]

Feeling God's love for us and desire for us to say "yes" encourages us to move from a stance of passivity to active co-creation with God. And because we are given free will, the divine never changes us without that "yes."

ADA MCKENZIE'S STORY
I'm 92 years old and I've attended Grace Lutheran Church for 38 years. I go to the early family service because I love to see the young people. I have many friends in other faith traditions; I

believe we are all one in the Spirit of God, all brothers and sisters together.

In 1943, our family was experiencing a great deal of anguish and we didn't know what to do about it. My husband, Gordon, was an alcoholic. He felt extremely remorseful about his addiction, yet was unable to control it.

I was an obstetrics nurse. One New Year's Day, I was on shift when a telephone call came in from my daughter. She said, "Mom, Dad's so sick, I don't think he's going to make it." I hung up the phone in despair. What could we do?

Just then, Dr. Buffam walked by and wished me "Happy New Year." I broke down. He listened and then asked if I would like him to go out to my husband right then. I was very grateful, but didn't know what he could do that we, his family, hadn't already tried. He left me for a few minutes and then returned with a Dr. McGill. I was told that Dr. McGill had a special interest in alcoholism and wanted to start a group in our city called Alcoholics Anonymous. I shared my pain with him.

A few hours later, I finished my shift and went home. Walking into the house, I could see Gordon and the two doctors still in conversation. As my dear husband looked up at me, his face shone with such a great relief. He never took another drink.

God gave us the people to help and offered the program that would save Gordon and the family. It wasn't a coincidence that the one doctor in our city who wanted to start an AA group was in the hospital with me on that New Year's Day. If I hadn't shared my pain with Dr. McGill, though, he wouldn't have been able to assist us.

Also, we had to agree to the guidance we received and do our part in the healing and growth. It is a partnership between us and the Holy Spirit. And, in AA, the partnership broadens. The community that develops is truly wonderful. Wounded people helping other wounded people.

Gordon and I were married 61 years. When he died, he had been sober and a member of AA for 45 years.

RT. REVEREND MICHELE FAVARGER'S STORY

Many years ago, I was ordained as a Wiccan Priestess through the Aquarian Tabernacle Church, having decided that this was my personal path of spirituality. After several years of practicing my faith as a private individual, I took the second level of dedication, which meant the focus of my spirituality would be moving from the private to the public realm.

I had not yet decided how I might best be of service to my community, when I was asked to perform a handfasting (a Wiccan wedding) for my Goddess daughter and her partner, who was an inmate at a federal prison. Because our church was not recognized by the provincial government, the ceremony had to be witnessed by a Marriage Commissioner.

Many hurdles had to be jumped to get permission to do the ceremony behind bars, and the prison's support was less than enthusiastic. When the day finally arrived, however, the beautiful ceremony appropriately reflected the spirituality of the couple.

Once the "religious" portion of the ceremony was completed, the Marriage Commissioner stepped forward as was expected, and everyone anticipated that the marriage register and license would be signed. Imagine our shock when he inquired as to who had his 90 bucks and then demanded that the couple remove their rings. The bride, a spunky young thing, promptly refused, as she was, in her view, already married. The Commissioner then proceeded to conduct his version of a marriage.

My question around what service I was to give to my community was suddenly very clear. It was like a light bulb turning on inside me. I was to work to have our faith and church recognized by our provincial government. The Gods had made their will known. Ignoring divine will wasn't an option. My only choice was to follow through.

As a result, I am now the Archpriestess of the Aquarian Tabernacle Church of Canada. Handfastings are now legally recognized in our province. I now work on a weekly basis with my Wiccan study group at that prison. Oh, yes, and the spunky young lady and her very successful husband have bought a house and are expecting their fourth child very soon.

These two stories show that the outcome of intentionally working with God is often vastly different than we could ever expect.

Love

God is love,
and those who abide in love abide in God,
and God abides in them
1 JOHN 4:16

Our urge for discernment often comes after a loving encounter, feeling touched by love or reaching out in love. Sometimes, discernment comes through love.

SANDY'S STORY

Sandy came to me for psychotherapy to help her heal after the death of her parents. As we worked together, it became clear that one of the issues making it difficult to accept their deaths and embrace life more fully was her spirituality. Sandy had had a number of mystical experiences that overwhelmed and confused her. She wanted to develop a relationship with this awesome God and yet was not clear about how to start.

As well as exploring psychological issues and concerns, we talked about her spiritual history and her image of God. Sandy tended to be extremely self-judgmental and she saw how this pattern negatively affected her emotional and spiritual life. One day, Sandy told me about the quiet voice that seemed to sit on her right shoulder. She had received encouragement from this voice when she was in a difficult situation the previous weekend. I asked her to describe the voice to me.

"Well, I hear it periodically, usually when I am having a painful or stressful time."

"Uh huh."

"It's always a deeply loving message. Encouragement, support, telling me I'm loved and cherished."

"Do you ever hear anything negative?" I asked.

"No." She replied.

As we continued our conversation, Sandy realized that she would never be able to give herself such unconditional love, especially during times of high stress. This was God. This awareness struck her so forcefully she cried with gratitude and awe for a long time.

In subsequent weeks, Sandy was able to be more receptive to God's yearning to connect with her in love. As she developed a more conscious, intentional relationship with God; her view of herself began to change. She started to see herself more as God did – as a cherished daughter who did not have to change to be acceptable. This had a positive impact on the grief work she was doing around her parents' deaths.

She also realized that God wanted to be a partner in her life. Now, sometimes the voice comes while she is in a discernment process; sometimes God draws her attention to a certain path through other means. The emotional flavor for her is always the same though; she feels led by Love.

Gratitude

Clouds hanging low in the sky.
Wind comes a circling by.
How can we savour the wonder of this day?

Laughter that dances on air.
If you had only one prayer.
Would that a thank you might be all you'd say.

Lay your burdens down.
Sing your own life's part.
And there where your treasure lies.
There is your heart.
LINNEA GOOD[46]

Many of the people I interviewed told me that they also see gratitude as an essential part of any spiritual practice, especially discernment. To feel grateful, we must acknowledge that another, whether God or one of God's creations, has done something that helps or delights us. Gratitude is a stance of appreciative receptivity. It accepts the reality that others can enter into our space and influence us to our benefit.

VIKTOR FRANKL'S STORY

Viktor Frankl worked as a psychotherapist with suicidal patients prior to the Second World War. He continued his work until 1942, when he and his wife and parents were deported to Nazi death camps. Viktor spent the next three years in four camps, not knowing the fate of his loved ones and undergoing much humiliation and brutality.

He later wrote *Man's Search for Meaning*, which describes his experiences in the camps and speaks of the importance of "meaning" in life. Those prisoners who were unable to develop and live a meaning that took their cruel reality into account, without losing their humanity, lost the will to live.

Prior to this excerpt, Viktor described the difficulty the prisoners had adjusting to liberation. "'Freedom' – we repeated to ourselves, and yet we could not grasp it. We had said this word so often during all the years we dreamed about It, that it had lost its meaning."[47]

Viktor needed help to move from this emotional numbness. Throughout his imprisonment, verses from scripture would come into his mind when he was trying to discern an attitudinal path that would help him through his ordeal. He recounts how he was guided at this time.

> One day, a few days after the liberation, I walked through the country past flowering meadows, for miles and miles, toward the market town near the camp. Larks rose to the sky and I could hear their joyous song. There was no one to be seen for miles around; there was nothing but the wide earth and sky and the lark's jubilation and the freedom of space. I stopped, looked around, and up to the sky – and then I went down on my knees. At that moment there was very little I knew of myself or of the world – I had but one sentence in mind – always the same: "I called to the Lord from my narrow prison and He answered me in the freedom of space."
>
> How long I knelt there and repeated this sentence, memory can no longer recall. But I know that on that day, in that hour, my new life started. Step for step I progressed, until I again became a human being. (Frankl, p. 111)

Viktor could not feel joy at the beauty of nature or at his new freedom. He could feel gratitude. And that movement toward God was all that was needed to start the healing.

Ripening discernment

*Like an archaeologist, the Spirit works within us
to uncover the wisdom and discernment buried deep within ourselves.*
DANNY E. MORRIS AND CHARLES M. OLSEN[48]

Most of the people I interviewed stressed that their story of discernment was only *one* way that they were called to understand God's will for them. As they became more aware of their constant, "hands-on" relationship with the All, they found guidance occurring more often and in many different ways. The familiarity of deep, long-term friendship encourages and makes possible an ease and sensitivity within our relationships with others, and with God.

For many, their discernment became less formal. At one point in writing this book, I was feeling gratitude for the multiplicity of ways in which we can discern. I imagined trying to hold all the methods as they were poured into my hands, to decide which one to use. I soon collapsed under the sheer number, surrendering my need to hold the best one. In my image, I then was moved beyond reliance on any one method. God will guide me to the most appropriate method at any particular time.

Here are some of the ways a discernment process can ripen over time.

KELLY'S STORY

My spiritual practices and ways of discerning have certainly changed over the years. I view human beings as uninflated balloons until we are filled with the breath of God. None of us know what our final shape will be. Early in my spiritual journey, I passionately called to God, "I'm willing to do anything to know you!" I threw myself at God, spending a lot of time reading and memorizing the Bible, praying two to three hours a day. I focused on God's Word to develop an understanding of God and of what God wanted me to do with my life.

I received many signs that God was providing for me. And I really wore myself down beating on heaven's door. I finally realized that I was talking a lot in this relationship and not listening much. I have a very strong ego. My knowledge of scripture was actually getting in the way. The Word was essential, and yet was only one of many ways to experience God.

Once I learned to listen, I didn't have to hold as tight to God and to what I was being given. I learned how to ask for what I needed and wanted. One day, in prayer, God said to me, "Don't whine; just ask!" Instead of taking a scripture reading as the sole source of a particular issue for me, I would use the Word as a starting point. I would ask God, "What do you have to say to me here?" Then I would ask specific yes or no questions, and wait for the answer.

For example, one day, I felt an inner urge to apologize. No idea why or to whom. As I asked my questions, the distinct impression of a person came into my mind. "Is it Mark?" The feeling of affirmation was a warmth in the center of my being. This byproduct of the Holy Spirit's presence felt like suddenly being plugged into a divine electrical current. There was also an understanding of what I was to apologize for. It's like God implants this; one moment I didn't know and the next moment I did.

Now I trust that God will tell me in the most appropriate manner what I am to do and how I am to go about it. It may be a dream that just doesn't leave me during the day or is reflected in my waking life. I hear a voice more often, now. Sometimes, in church, I will receive a message for an individual or the congregation and I need to speak it out.

As a Pentecostal pastor, many people come to me wanting to discern God's will for them. I try to help them find how they are being called. One method I have used, to get ego out of the way, is a group one. A number of us meet with a question or concern held in our minds. We do not tell each other what our focus is. Then we pray together. We each ask the Spirit to give us a mental symbol that will help us with our concern.

Then, each of us shares the symbol we have been given. Frequently, the Spirit gives one person an image, such as a fence, that won't resonate with anything in their life. As they share the symbol with the others, one person will say, "Oh, that's for me." As they explain their question, we can all see the guidance they are being given.

LINDA KAVELIN POPOV'S STORY

As co-founder of The Virtues Project™, I conduct many weekend workshops and retreats. At one retreat about 12 years ago, I was meditating early one Saturday morning. I had met my group the evening before and was eager to continue our personal exploration and growth process. During meditation, some words floated into my consciousness. I then "saw" one of the women on the retreat and knew the words were for her. Then more words came for another group member. I went in search of note-cards and discovered a box of varied cards I had purchased years before. I chose a card for each woman in the retreat and wrote what I had heard Spirit say for her. When the women read their cards, they were deeply touched and affirmed in their path.

I continued to receive messages, always supportive and full of love, during other retreats. So, now, the rare times I facilitate private retreats, I collect beautiful greeting cards as I am led to them, and, during the second morning of a retreat, I lay the cards out on the bed. Then I pray and follow the guidance that gives me the appropriate message and appropriate card for each participant. Frequently participants are astounded at how I knew an issue or concern they were struggling with. I didn't know. God knows and uses me as a hollow reed. The retreatants' discernment process is enhanced and I become aware of some aspect of them to be more sensitive to throughout our time together.

I was raised in the Baha'i faith. Baha'is have a very active approach to prayer and guidance. Reading sacred writings each day is an important part of it. Communion with God is extremely important and this orients us to service. A Baha'i teaching is that work done in the spirit of service is the highest form of prayer. Clarifying and nurturing our unique gifts helps shape our service.

Since I was a child, I have felt God's deep love holding me. There was a sense of God's Presence around me, all the time. I am led to discern Divine will for me through many methods. Sometimes there are words, like someone is talking very clearly to me. After struggling for some time with the fatigue and other symptoms of Post-Polio Syndrome, I heard one day, "I will give you ten rules for health. Write them down and follow them." These rules have helped me enormously to restore my energy.

Some time ago, I made a vision quest, a First Nations discernment process. During that profound experience, I encountered my sacred animal. Fox shows me the wisdom of sitting contemplatively and then, when opportunity comes, jumping on it. At times, God gives me other visions to guide me into the right path. My brother and I had the same vision in meditation when we asked ten years ago what we should do with *The Virtue's Guide*, the book we wrote with my husband, Dan, which started The Virtues Project™.

We both heard Spirit say, "First Nations first." The first call we had that day was from Fran Dick of the Tsawataineuk First Nation saying, "Bring this wisdom of virtues to our people." Synchronicity often follows prayer, giving such awesome confirmation! We spent the first few years of The Virtues Project working with First Nations across Canada.

My dreams can also help my discernment process. I know that God wants to continue and deepen our connection and will always touch and guide me in many ways.

You may find it interesting to look at how you have been given guidance over the years, whether you were aware of being in relationship with God or not. Remember five or six decisions you made and look for evidence of divine presence. If it's not immediately clear, look for who or what God worked through to provide you with love, acceptance, or support.

PART TWO

METHODS

Experiencing God within

A person blended into God does not disappear.
He, or she, is just completely soaked in God's qualities.
RUMI[49]

At one time or another in their lives, many people have had an experience within their bodies of being touched by the All. For some, their most frequent connection with God is an inner one.

THOMAS MERTON'S STORY

In his book *The Seven Storey Mountain*, Merton describes the first time God called him to attend a Catholic Mass.

> I will not easily forget how I felt that day. First, there was this sweet, strong, gentle, clean urge in me which said, "Go to Mass! Go to Mass!" It was something quite new and strange, this voice that seemed to prompt me, this firm, growing interior conviction of what I needed to do. It had a suavity, a simplicity about it that I could not easily account for. And when I gave in to it, it did not exult over me, and trample me down in its raging haste to land its prey, but it carried me forward serenely and with purposeful direction.[50]

Like Thomas Merton, many people know that such an experience does not originate in themselves; it is divine. And yet it is often difficult to adequately describe how they know. Using words like "awesome," "overwhelming," "a love beyond anything I could imagine," gives us only an inkling of the reality.

A number of the stories throughout this book mention these experiences and yet a large volume could not encompass the variety of divine touches. Ignatius of Loyola kept track of his inner experiences of God in his journal. They take up many pages.

God may be felt as a sensation: strong energy flowing up, down, throughout the body; a warmth, an electrical charge. God may come as emotion: melting love, joy, delight. God may speak in a still, small voice that is heard or sensed. God may be a "knowing" in the gut or the head.

A woman in one of my workshops spoke of a time she was "sunk deep" in contemplative prayer. Candace experienced a "rich, refreshing" taste in her mouth. This taste recurred quite frequently, at first in prayer and then during her daily life. She knew this taste was of God. One day, she was trying to decide between two options that seemed equally appealing and beneficial to her. As she thought of one, she experienced the taste. When she thought of the other, it disappeared. Candace took this as a sign to start down the first path. Here are some other stories of God experienced within.

LAURA'S STORY

It was the morning of Sigrid's memorial service and I was in a panic. It was so important for Sigrid that the music be just right, that we had recorded her singing before the terminal illness had progressed too far. Sigrid recorded most of the songs for her own service, but she also wanted and trusted me to sing. It was to be a piece we had always done as a duet. And now I would be singing solo, *a cappella*, knowing that I would never see my beloved friend and music partner again.

So I fled to the beach, where I have always experienced the comfort of God. As I walked, I remembered how Sigrid and I had first connected: singing together in the waiting room of the hospital hours before the surgery she would undergo to try to stop her cancer; and the many hours afterward – leading the "pre-game warm-up" singing at church, vesper services, doing women's spiritual weekend retreats, putting together children's songs for summer camps. All of the work we did together was centered around the development of our own form of faith and closely tied to music and nature. Much of the planning for this work had taken place at her piano, over our guitars, and on walks along this very beach.

On this same beach, Sigrid had taught me to find agates.

These smooth chunks of quartz that become translucent as they are ground down by the action of sand and water were a powerful spiritual image for her. And every time she walked the beach, she found an agate! "I don't collect agates," I remember telling her. "I collect eagles." They are a potent spiritual symbol for me and always seem to be present when I need them.

But Sigrid was determined to broaden my horizons by showing me that looking down was as important as looking up. She taught me to find agates by walking toward the light. She said I would see them before me, because the light will shine through them. "Always follow and trust the light," she said.

No more gathering agates with Sigrid! How could I sing, in just a few hours with this lump in my throat! Panic rose in me. The weather in the back dykes was as turbulent as my internal state. There seemed to be no separation from inside and outside. Tears streaming down my face, I found myself calling aloud to God for comfort and guidance.

Then I looked up and saw an eagle. She was being buffeted by the wind, flapping her wings hard as she slowly moved forward. Her sharp cries sounded irritated. "Boy, sister, do I know how you feel," I called to her. Just then she caught an updraft and swiftly rose, smoothly and effortlessly. Her call was clear and strong and joyous. Still in communion with her, my spirits rose as well. Anxiety was transformed into calm. I felt euphoric. Every cell of my body felt larger. I knew God had answered my call. I knew that Sigrid was safe at home, healed and whole and that I would be more than able to sing at her service. I knew that I would be able to sing wherever I was needed.

I sang my heart out at the memorial service. As people were filing into the church, Sigrid's sons held large baskets of agates and invited each mourner to choose a stone to remember her by. People held the stones in their hands and felt the growing warmth and were reminded of the light that Sigrid believed was available for everyone to follow. That service was a deeply spiritual experience for many people.

Strangely enough, that's when I began to leave structured group worship. I had always been very active in the church. Besides attending and singing in the choir, leading the "pre-game warm-up" and reading scripture, I had served on committees as needed. There had been no thought of leaving my spiritual home.

Yet in the weeks after the powerful memorial service, I felt the divine calling to me in every place *but* the church. I was being called out and away. But called to what? Another friend, a woman who had been very close to Sigrid's spiritual awakening, was also trying to discern the path God was calling her to. She and I began to walk the beach nearly every day, sharing our spiritual questions and concerns. Increasingly, I was aware of the sacredness of the beach, of all creation. Experiencing God potently in every thing and every moment. I realized that I had been focused too much on God in formalized worship within a particular building.

Since I was a little child, I have had a physical sensation of the Holy. God speaks to me in a combination of sensation and awareness. I know the path God wants me to take when I experience a marvelous enlivening feeling that makes my body seem larger. Frequently, there is an electric current that starts at my feet and radiates through my body. This is accompanied by an awareness that I feel in my heart. This discernment experience is most common for me in nature. I didn't understand as a child, but I know now that everyone is invited to have a personal relationship with the divine and that there are many paths leading to the same place.

It took a while to discover what God had in store for me. Now the time I used to spend volunteering in and attending church is given to a volunteer music ministry with seniors in care homes. I find that there is a great sharing of love with these elders. Often, the people with Alzheimer's disease don't remember my name or even what they had for lunch. But they do remember the lyrics to songs they loved "way back when." They revel in the freedom of returning to their past and knowing their way around in it. We share music and love in the moment. The sharing with these people is as natural as walking on the beach. I'm able to look for the light in them and the divine blesses me with the gift of seeing it. For me, for now, that is worship.

HILDEGARD'S STORY

"And again I heard a voice from heaven instructing me thus; and it said, 'Write in this way, just as I tell you.'"[51] Hildegard of Bingen (1098–1179) was given many visions by the Holy Spirit and heard this call: "commit to permanent record for the benefit of humankind, what you see with your inner eyes and perceive with the inner ears of your soul so that, through these things, people may come to know their Creator and not recoil from worshipping him with the reverence due to him." (Bowie and Davies, p. 90) So she wrote. She described herself in her visions as "fully awake in body and mind – and not in dreams, nor in ecstasy." (Bowie and Davies, p. 91)

Hildegard said she had experienced visions for as long as she could remember. When only three, she "saw so great a brightness that my soul trembled." (Bowie and Davies, p. 20) The visions continued all her life and gave her information and direction about how to give this information to the world. She described seeing a non-spatial light, "the reflection (or shadow) of the living light." This light would produce images, sometimes accompanied by a voice which addressed her in Latin. (Bowie and Davies, p. 20)

Hildegard wrote a number of books, 27 songs and the music to go with them, and numerous letters. Given by her parents at age eight to a Benedictine monastery as an oblate, Hildegard later became a Benedictine nun. In her 60s, she was directed by her visions to go on a preaching tour, a very unusual occupation for a woman of her time.

MOTHER TERESA'S STORY

As a 12-year-old growing up in Albania, Agnes already knew God was calling her to a religious life. Inspired by letters from missionaries, she was completely convinced that this was the path God wanted her to take. So, at 18, she entered the Congregation of Loreto nuns, knowing they worked in Bengal.

When her novitiate was completed, Agnes made her first vows and took the religious name "Teresa," after St. Therese of Liseaux, patroness of missionaries. St. Therese's spiritual path was known as the "little way," because she encouraged growing closer to God through humility and service through the ordinary tasks of everyday life.

This way resonated very strongly with Teresa. And yet she found herself, as a Loretto sister, teaching history and geography in the Congregation's high school in Calcutta for 17 years. All around the beautiful grounds of the convent was the poverty and attendant illness of the local people. Teresa's heart went out to them. "I knew where I belonged, but I didn't know how to get there," she said many years later.

God showed her the way. She described it as a "call within a call." It came as a clear message as she was traveling to Darjeeling by train to make a retreat, September 10, 1946. "I was to leave the convent and help the poor while living among them."[52] Many people asked her over the years to describe more fully that communication from God. She always refused. "The call of God to be a Missionary of Charity is the hidden treasure for me, for which I have sold all to purchase it. You remember in the Gospel, what the man did when he found the hidden treasure – he hid it. This is what I want to do for God." (Spink, p. 21)

Felt experiences of the divine are not rewards for good behavior or outcomes of advanced spiritual development. Some people whose lives or writing have inspired millions have never had such experiences. God invites us to the methods that take our personal needs into account.

Prayer

Prayer cannot change the unalterable Truth,
nor can prayer alone give an understanding of Truth;
but prayer, coupled with a fervent habitual desire to know
and do the will of God, will bring us into all Truth.
MARY BAKER EDDY[53]

Any communication with the divine is prayer. Often, we only think of prayer as petition – asking for needs and desires to be met. In her book *Pray Like Hell*, Maxine Outlaw suggests we frequently treat God as if Holy Mystery were a giant ATM machine. We put our prayer credit card in and expect to get the response we have specified. Broadening our view and practice of prayer deepens relationship with God. It can also help discernment to be more effective, because putting our question or concern into words often clarifies it.

UMM-UL-QASIM'S STORY

A devout Muslim woman, Umm-ul-Qasim told me of her discernment around her son's marriage. The young man desired to marry and told his family what qualities he was wishing for in a wife. Some family members knew a young woman who was also wishing to marry and who they felt would be compatible. The young couple was pleased with the information they received about each other, agreed to marry, and a wedding date was set. During the month preceding the wedding, Umm-ul-Qasim added a special prayer of guidance to the obligatory *salah*, the prayer sequence which Muslims repeat five times daily. She also said this prayer at other times she felt were appropriate.

A prayer for seeking Allah's counsel, the *Istikhdra*, is found in the book *Citadel of the Believer: Invocations from Qur'an and Sunnah*. In it, Jobin bin Abdullah (may Allah be pleased with him) recounts that as a companion of the Prophet Muhammad (peace be upon him) he was taught to seek

Allah's counsel in all matters, saying, "Whoever seeks the counsel of the Creator will not regret it."

> Oh Allah, I seek the counsel of Your knowledge, and I seek the help of Your omnipotence and I beseech Your magnificant grace. Surely You are capable and I am not. Surely You know and I know not, and You are the Knower of the Unseen. Oh Allah, surely You know, so if this matter _____ is good for me, in my religion and in my life and for my welfare in the Hereafter – then ordain it for me and make it easy for me and bless me in it. And if this matter is bad for me – in my religion and in my life and for my welfare in the life to come – then distance it from me, and distance me from it, and ordain for me what is good wherever it is to be found and help me to be content with it.[54]

Umm-ul-Qasim told me that during the repetition of this prayer she felt an increasing sense of peace and knew that this path was the right one for her beloved son and his intended wife.

SHOGHI EFFENDI'S STORY

Shoghi Effendi Rabbani was the Guardian of the Baha'i faith, the central figure of the faith after the passing of his grandfather, Abdu'l-Baha. He was a young man of 21 attending Oxford University in England, far from his family living at the Baha'i World Center in Haifa, Israel, when the shocking news of the passing of his beloved grandfather came by cable.

His life changed forever when he learned that in the Will and Testament of Abdu'l-Baha, he had been appointed the Guardian of the Faith. His great-grandfather, Baha'u'llah, had been the founder of this new religion, which began in 1844. Shoghi Effendi was so grieved by the loss of his grandfather and daunted by the enormous responsibilities of stewarding this world faith that he retreated to the mountains of Switzerland. He hiked and prayed in solitude to gain strength and discernment about how to go on with his life. He remained in his role as guardian until his death at the age of 57.

He described the following method of discernment: I have placed the key points in italics.

1st step: *Pray and meditate* about it. Use the prayers of the Manifestations (Christ, Buddha, Baha'u'llah, Muhammad etc.) as they have the greatest power. Then remain in the silence of *contemplation* for a few minutes.

2nd step: *Arrive at a decision* and hold this. This decision is usually born during the contemplation. It may seem almost impossible of accomplishment but if it seems to be as answer to a prayer or way of solving the problem, then immediately take the next step.

3rd step: *Have determination* to carry the decision through. Many fail here. The decision, budding into determination, is blighted and instead becomes a wish or a vague longing. When determination is born, immediately take the next step.

4th step: *Have faith and confidence* that the power will flow through you, the right way will appear, the door will open, the right thought, the right message, the right principle, or the right book will be given to you. Have confidence and the right thing will come to your need. Then, as you rise from prayer, take at once the fifth step.

5th step: *Act as though it had all been answered.* Then act with tireless, ceaseless energy. And, as you act, you, yourself, will become a magnet, which will attract more power to your being, until you become an unobstructed channel for the Divine power to flow through you.[55]

Praying takes many forms: from highly structured words, to a silent listening. If you feel called to explore prayer methods more fully, books, workshops, or spiritual directors can teach you a variety of ways to pray.

Scripture

So shall my word be that goes out from my mouth;
it shall not return to me empty,
but it shall accomplish that which I purpose,
and succeed in the thing for which I sent it.
ISAIAH 55:11

In their daily spiritual practice, Sikhs use a discernment method. It is called *Vaak Lao*, "Taking the Word." *Vaak Lao* is also used for special occasions: at death, initiation, and marriage, as well as when naming a child. Parmajit (S.) Attariwala talked with me about this process and showed me the video of the wedding of his daughter Babena, and son-in-law Inderjit. God's blessing and word of guidance for their marriage is recorded for all time.

PARMAJIT'S STORY

In 1469, our founder, Guru Nanak, was inspired by God to begin a religion of human equality which views people of all faiths as children of God. There is one God, who is the Truth and the only Reality. A Sikh's goal is union with God. The fifth Guru compiled hymns from many sources that reflected God's awesome presence. It became the Adi Granth, our book of scripture. The Adi Granth contains over 5,000 hymns from Sikh Gurus, Hindu Brahmins, Hindu Low Caste (Shudras), Sufis, and Muslims.

The tenth Guru said that there would be no more human gurus for Sikhs. From that time on, the scripture has been Guru Adi Granth. All hymns in our scriptures are written in traditional classical ragas and can be sung. Singing aligns all aspects of the worshiper to God's presence and will. When we are more aligned to God, the answer to a problem or question may become clearer.

In our community worship and in individual prayer times, we start with the following prayer:

> *To Thee my Lord, I offer this prayer.*
> *To Thee I owe my body and soul.*
> *Thou art our Mother and Father, we are Thy children.*
> *It is by Thy Grace that we are given the countless comforts of life.*
> *No one can fathom Thy limits.*
> *Thou, the Highest of the High.*
> *The universe is a marvel of Thy Creation.*
> *Its working reflects Thy wishes.*
> *Only Thou knowest the limits of Thine grand design.*
> *Nanak, Thy servitor, is forever willing to sacrifice his all for Thee.*[56]

Then the Adi Granth is opened, allowing divine inspiration to choose the page. The hymn at the top of the left page is read. God's words are then held in our hearts for the rest of that day. They provide support and guidance.

On the morning of the wedding, my wife's family came to dress and otherwise prepare Babena. Anyone who feels called by God to Vaak Lao, can open the Adi Granth for a particular occasion. Babena's grandmother took the Word. The hymn spoke of God's name being very glorious, as the color red is glorious, and asks that God's name permeate everyone in the community. In our culture, the color red is associated with great happiness. A truly wonderful blessing and guidance for this marriage.

But that wasn't all. During the wedding ceremony, Babena's uncle felt called to open the Adi Granth. Remember, there are over 5,000 hymns. He opened to the exact same reading!

JOY WRIGHT'S STORY

Being born into a family of Christian Scientists, I grew up deeply influenced by the Holy Bible and by *Science and Health: With Key to the Scriptures*, written by our founder, Mary Baker Eddy. I often find that when I am wanting to discern which option God desires for me or when I find myself in a difficult situation and start to go down the wrong path, a piece of scripture or a quotation from *Science and Health* will come into my mind, directing, comforting, and encouraging me. Sometimes, God speaks directly to me.

For example, after a long illness my husband passed away, when our youngest sons were 11 and 13. Right on the heels of being informed of his passing, I experienced a sense of loss. I said to myself, "You've lost your husband. Your children have lost their father." I immediately heard a response, "You've lost nothing. I am your father; I am your All." I experienced a deep confidence and a sense that "All is well," not just for me and the children, but also for my husband.

I could see and feel that my husband was an expression of God's love for me. My husband was gone, God's love wasn't. By seeing how that love was still being expressed in my life, I could find my way to healing.

Once I was accepting of this change of perception, the following quotation came into my mind. It was a great comfort throughout the normal grieving process:

Divine Love always has met and always will meet every human need. It is not well to imagine that Jesus demonstrated the divine power to heal only for a select number or for a limited period of time, since to all mankind and in every hour, divine Love supplies all good.[57]

Soon after, I had a very concrete decision to make, one that I would previously have made with my husband. My old car was on its last legs. I knew there was a lot of work to do on it. It was clear that a new car was needed. My choice was between a used car which would initially save me money, or a new car which would probably give me less trouble in the long run. I talked to my daughter and she gave me the name of a friend who worked in an automobile dealership.

After introductions, the salesman said, "So, what color car would you like?" Oh dear, he was seeing me as a woman who was only interested in appearances. I firmly told him, "I want a car that will run well." He showed me a number of used and new models. Even after seeing them, I was still uncertain which way to go.

Then the following pieces of scripture came into my mind accompanied by a feeling of rightness, confidence, and well-being.

A good measure, pressed down, shaken together, running over,
will be put into your lap: for the measure you give
will be the measure you get back.
LUKE 6:38

You anoint my head with oil; my cup overflows. Surely goodness
and mercy shall follow me all the days of my life.
PSALM 23

So I looked more closely at the new cars and found a station wagon, which would be very useful ferrying the boys from one sports game to another. It turned out to be a demonstration model with only 5,000 km and a very good warranty. So I got my new car, at a less expensive price.

My next choice was to pay outright (I did have insurance money I could use) or pay by installments, which was more practical. I heard a combination of scripture and God speaking to me directly: "Sufficient unto the day. The need is for now, the supply is now. Tomorrow will take care of itself." I purchased the station wagon outright. Within a year, the same amount of money was back in my bank account.

VANESSA HAMMOND'S STORY

Often, when I'm trying to decide which direction I want to go in – such as phoning a friend, or in another direction I'm not so keen on, such as tidying or filing papers – a song or piece of scripture floats into my mind, giving me direction and, if it's the task I don't want to do, support. My goal would be to do everything with God's guidance. Although I often fail to listen, I believe

God is always telling me which way to go. Tuning in to the song or scripture quote brings God's will to my awareness.

If you are using scripture as a discernment method, don't just stay with the first meaning that comes to your mind. This may be ego's definition. Let the reading work and ferment in you like yeast, over a period of time. Your guidance will be refined and confirmed. As it says in Hebrews 4:12, "The word of God is alive and active."

Worship

People gathered for genuine worship
are like a heap of fresh and burning coals
warming one another as a great strength,
freshness and vigor of life flows to all.
ISAAC PENINGTON

If attending corporate worship is a part of a person's spiritual practice, it is natural to bring questions and concerns to the service. Sometimes, God speaks to us through some aspect of the worship service, before we're even consciously aware of a need for direction. At other times, we will bring a clear discernment issue to worship.

The various sections of many types of worship services provide different ways to hold our question and ourselves up to God. Father Ted Dobson, author of *Say but the Word: How the Lord's Supper Can Transform Your Life*, speaks about the healing and transformative power of the Christian Eucharist, or Holy Communion.

I have adapted his material to view this worship service as a method for discernment. The basic principles for discernment during worship will be the same for other Christian services that do not include Holy Communion and for services of other faith traditions.

CLARE'S STORY

I met Clare at a workshop where she told me how important Eucharist is to her. She attends Mass a number of times a week. Recently she was trying to decide between two equally appealing courses of action. I have used her story to illustrate my adaptation of Dobson's work.

Prior to worship

Clarify the issue as much as you can. I suggest people try to give it a short title or sum it up in a sentence. It is then easier to hold in our hearts and minds. Viewing the issue as a symbol may also be useful. Clare thought of her question as a tightly closed rosebud, full of potential and mystery. Throughout the Eucharist, she repeatedly brought this image to the forefront of her mind. As I describe the general process, we will follow Clare's discernment.

Once you have clarified and named your issue, collect yourself physically, emotionally, mentally, and spiritually, so that you are as present as possible to yourself and to God. Clare did an internal check and found that her body was quite tight and her emotions in turmoil about her impending decision. She breathed more deeply and imagined herself tenderly cradling her rosebud. She asked God to give her patience; she wanted to love her rosebud into opening, not force it open. Checking internally again, Clare was aware of a centering down; her body was more relaxed and she felt a peaceful anticipation.

The Opening Rite

Worship begins with praise. Praise opens us to the awesomeness of God and of our relationship with the divine. The Quakers define worship as "to love with wonder." During this time of praise, and throughout the rest of the service, we hold our question or concern in our consciousness, asking, not demanding, to receive the guidance that God wishes us to have. Dobson says that praise makes us as vulnerable as possible to God. This vulnerability helps us let go of those aspects of ourselves that are making it difficult to hear God's will for us.

Clare could enter more fully into the opening song and prayers because of the preparation she had just done. She imagined herself joyfully holding her imaginary rose up to God, aware of God's great love and care.

The Penitential Rite

During the time of confession, "ask God's forgiveness regarding any self-ishness or other sinfulness involved with this issue."[58] Be aware of God's unconditional love, forgiveness, and longing for you to be healed. Allow yourself to give God any shame or embarrassment you hold about your question or issue.

As Clare thought of the times she had stepped away from God during the past week, she realized her ego's need to make a decision had some-times resulted in irritability and her ignoring the needs of others. She started to feel ashamed of herself: an old, old pattern. Fortunately, she had worked on this pattern for some time and was able to intentionally let God's healing love and forgiveness enter and transform the tight feeling of shame in her chest.

The Liturgy of the Word

When God's Word is read, we may find it addressing our issue. We may also find it speaking about something else in our lives. "The same truth spoken at the same time can, under the guidance of the Spirit, enter each open heart precisely in the way that heart needs to hear it. The only pre-disposition necessary is to be expecting God's Word to make a difference when we hear it." (Dobson, p. 23–24) An attitude of receptivity without assumptions will allow us to expect God's Word to live within us, without trying to control how it will live.

The parable of the "Good Samaritan" was a favorite of Clare's and she enjoyed the sermon which gave her some insights into her life in general. There didn't seem to be anything in it, though, about her issue.

The Liturgy of the Eucharist

The word Eucharist comes from the Greek prefix *eu*, meaning "good," and the Greek *charis*, meaning "beautiful" or "gift." Placed together these ideas have come to mean "thanksgiving." Unite all aspects of your issue to the bread and wine during the preparation of these gifts and their consecration.

"As the bread and wine are transformed and made sacred, so are we transformed and made sacred, if we unite ourselves consciously and prayerfully with these symbols of the sacrifice." (Dobson, p. 31) Align yourself with the sacrifice God made for us through Jesus. "The meaning of [sacrifice] is probably most clearly shown by the root words from which it comes: *sacrum facere*, which in Latin literally mean 'to make sacred' or 'to consecrate.'...To sacrifice, then, in its root form, means to make something sacred by giving it to God, in such a way that it changes, and at least feels as if it were being destroyed." (Dobson, p. 12–13)

Clare, who had really hoped to have a "blinding flash of guidance" during the Liturgy of the Word, realized that her body was tense again and she was feeling some anxiety. She consciously gave this restricted feeling to God, along with herself and her question.

Prayers of the People

This part of the worship service may be placed before or after Communion, depending on the denomination. Realizing that others also have concerns, sufferings, and decisions to make, encourages a solidarity with others and may put our own issue in perspective. Clare, remembering her daughter's difficult transition to a new school that year, asked the congregation to pray for her.

The Lord's Prayer or the "Our Father"

"Thy will be done." The prayer taught by Jesus contains all aspects of our relationship with God: praise, thanksgiving, longing for closer connection, agreement to work in partnership to bring God's Kingdom and will to earth, petition for sustenance and forgiveness, and acknowledgment of God's status as glorious and powerful.

Clare was fully present to worship at this point and experienced gratitude that God would want her as partner in the divine plan for peace and harmony in the world. She did not consciously think of her own issue.

Passing the Peace

During the Passing of the Peace, we open more fully to the others who are worshiping with us. "To the degree to which we are intending to live in deep relationship with Christ, then, we will also then be willing to come into union with others, simply because that is the way He lives." (Dobson, p. 46)

During the Passing of the Peace, Clare "looked" at her rosebud and saw that it was now partially opened. She realized that of the two paths she was contemplating, one would bring more peace in her family's life. The other way was one of great disruption, yet it had the appeal of newness and challenge. Along with this realization came a feeling of "rightness" and as she shook hand after hand, this rightness grew.

Receiving Communion

Dobson says that Jesus used a custom derived from ancient Judaism, when the people renewed their promise to obey the Mosaic Law by eating the sacrificial lamb during Passover, to have us remember and unite with him. As we receive Communion, we eat and are eaten. God gives to us and we give to God.

We "are receiving into [our hearts] everyone else who has participated in the Eucharist" (Dobson, p. 120) and also all of God's creation throughout our world. Allowing a feeling of union with all creation can encourage a more holistic awareness of the implications of our issue or question. Clare imagined her partially opened rose entering the bread and the wine. As she said, "Amen," "So be it," she agreed to walk the path to which she felt God was calling her.

Dismissal, Benediction

Here we give thanks for what we have received during the time of corporate worship and receive blessings for our continued journey. Clarity about our issue for discernment may not yet have "bubbled to the surface" of our awareness. This is quite common and pushing at it will not help. Cultivating the attitude that we have already been given that which we asked for will allow us to go forth with gratitude and optimism. Being receptive to the diverse ways God could enlighten us to our path will encourage a wider vision.

Clare made her thanks and went out to walk her path. She shared with family and friends the discernment she had made. On the way home, she bought a rosebud that was just opening, as a concrete symbol of her decision. She later dried the petals and put them in her journal.

QUAKER WORSHIP SERVICES

The Society of Friends, or Quakers, conduct their corporate worship as discernment sessions. The congregation sits in silence, all senses attuned to the presence of the Holy Spirit. The silence is only broken if an individual feels led by Spirit to share an insight, piece of information, etc. This is called vocal ministry. However the urge to speak is experienced, it is expected that the individual receiving it will go through an internal process of discernment to differentiate their own ego desires and needs from that small, still voice within that is Spirit. An individual worshiper may also experience a leading from Spirit that is for themselves alone, not to be shared.

During the silence, the focus is on God. If the mind wanders, it is gently brought back to this focus. Patricia Loring says,

> Some feel that the refocusing itself is of central importance in worship. The repeated inner choice to come back to God, the practice of returning again and again to the Center, the iterated affirmation of the desire to listen in faithfulness, can form a habit of the heart that we can carry out of the time of worship. It can bring worship into the dailiness of all life, erasing the distinction between the secular and the sacred.[59]

Loring views individual and corporate worship as centering on listening. There is, however, a difference in the directionality of that listening. In true corporate worship,

> we listen for what Spirit is bringing forth from us as a body, for what new thing God is bringing forth within us corporately, for how our communal life may be of service to God... Together, we may come to a deeper sense of the gifts, trials and purposes of being drawn together in this particular meeting, at this time." (Loring, p. 23)

A spiritual fruit of such receptive listening, *gathering*, is experienced at some Quaker meetings. Gathering is "the felt union of the spiritual community in the Love, Life and Power of God." (Loring, p. 2) Some of the Friends I have spoken with tell me with awe of the profound feeling of interconnectedness there is in a gathered meeting, as Spirit speaks the same message to the open hearts and minds of the worshipers.

Reading

Ultimately, what makes reading devotional
is a mysterious fusion in the grace of God
of the content and our intention to be opened to guidance.
PATRICIA LORING[60]

One of the most commonly mentioned discernment methods seems to be finding the quotation or book that provides needed guidance or clarification.

PAUL TAYLOR'S STORY

Paul practices ministry in the United Church of Canada and has an interest in rummaging around in the hidden, forgotten, and ignored treasures of the Christian tradition.

Since I was very young, I have felt that God provides for me. Over the years, I have come to recognize how a certain book, sermon, or conversation has led me to deepen my commitment to God. Recognizing where God's will is leading in the present is an intuitive act, but I know that I am on track when I feel that an action or a decision is filling me with energy and vitality. Similarly, when I am missing what God wants me to pay attention to (which is often), I feel disorganized and lacking energy.

I try to keep track of these leads, nuggets, or clues in my journal. Recently, I had sensed that I needed to pay attention to how I speak.

I had a feeling that there was much more for me to learn about communicating God's grace, and began to watch for what might come my way. Over some weeks, I was led to nuggets in book after book until I came across a statement that really rang home.

[O]ne draws the hidden meaning from the literal sense of the biblical text, just as honey is made to flow from the honeycomb or as Moses drew water from the rock.[61]

This passage would have carried great weight for me at any time, but as I was reading I happened to be eating – honeycomb with toast! Earlier that week I had purchased honeycomb, something I had not done before. This convergence underlined the connection that had been growing through my reading: spiritual speaking is the expression of a personal integration of God's grace discovered in the act of spiritual reading. Now to put it into practice.

MAHATMA GANDHI'S STORY

In Gandhi's magazine *Young India*, of August 6, 1925, he wrote of the importance of scripture in his life. "When doubts haunt me, when disappointments stare me in the face, and I see not one ray of hope on the horizon, I turn to the Bhagavad-Gita, and find a verse to comfort me; and I immediately begin to smile in the midst of overwhelming sorrow." Gandhi spoke of the Gita as his "spiritual reference book" and attempted to live his life in accordance with the guidance he received from it.

The Bhagavad-Gita was not his only spiritual reference book, however. Gandhi read the holy writings of many faith traditions. One of his favorite guiding principles was the Christian "Sermon on the Mount," which "went straight to my heart" and which "delighted" him.

Gandhi also received guidance from other reading. He described the effect *Unto This Last*, a book by John Ruskin, had on him. "That book marked the turning point of my life." Louis Fischer, in his biography *Gandhi: His Life and Message for the World*, wrote that a passage in Ruskin "crystallized his determination" to buy a farm and live more simply.

Fischer described Gandhi as "a creative reader, he co-authored the impression a book made on him."[62]

Discerning his path through the divine guidance he received from his reading, Gandhi was transformed from a young lawyer so shy he could not speak out in court, to a highly vocal advocate for non-violence, Indian independence, and interfaith tolerance. He regularly read from the holy scriptures of other faith traditions during his Hindu prayer services. The bullets that killed him came from the gun of a Hindu who felt threatened by Gandhi's prayer that people of all religions live in harmony.

Sometimes, as happened with Mahatma Gandhi, a reading that "hits home" is how God gets our attention when we don't even realize a path needs to be taken or a decision needs to be made.

Writing

Try and be a sheet of paper with nothing on it.
Be a spot of ground where nothing is growing,
where something might be planted,
a seed, possibly, from the Absolute.
RUMI[63]

Whether the end result is poetry or prose, many people feel inspired to use writing as a medium for spiritual exploration, clarification, and the sharing of insights. These three storytellers are called to discernment through the written word.

STEPHEN BERER'S STORY

I see Jewish discernment revolving around the issue of how to be in relationship with G-d. We are all unique and therefore each of us needs to find our own path into this relationship. Poetry has been a very potent discernment tool for me since I was 20 years old, although I hadn't planned it that way.

At 20, I had had enough experience with society's judgment of the Jewish people to feel that being a Jew was to live with an intolerable burden and a deep shame. It was at this point that I denied I was Jewish to anyone who asked. I told myself G-d did not exist. I thought I was alone in the world, relying on my own powers.

In 1972, I left university with an interdisciplinary degree that combined psychology, mythic poetry, and social anthropology. It is humorous now to look back and see how I tried to take the sacred out of everything. I even read the Prophets as interesting literature.

I was denying my spirituality; I was denying G-d; I was denying being a Jew. Then the poetry started. I would experience a compelling image or a line from a text. It stayed with me, inviting me to move into it, to develop a relationship with it, to keep working it until I had written it correctly. Once I opened to the image, information came out in a stream that was too powerful to dam.

Looking back, I can see that the poetry was very spiritual right from the start. Yet I would have vehemently denied it, if anyone had been so bold as to point it out. I remember having many arguments with my roommates who were very spiritual. I always took the side of psychology, not realizing that psychology and spirituality can be compatible.

After graduating, I moved to Cape Cod and looked after a beautiful old waterfront home. There I wrote poetry for a year. The tides brought the poetry to me every single day. It was a special time. I can see now that the process of working with the images, discerning what to write, was really discerning how to be in relationship with G-d. The finished piece of poetry would have a certain elegance, a lucidity, complexity and simplicity that was beyond my powers. As I read it over, there would be a giddiness in my whole body and the thought, "Wow, I can't believe I could have written that."

The poetry opened me to spiritual questions, to issues of healing and growth. Looking back, I can chart the course of my spiritual development; the poetry always about three steps ahead of me, leading and luring me on. In 1986 or so, I began a poem about an angel of God coming to earth (personified as Ertha) to lift her from her inconscience. The poem is entitled, *The Song ov Elmallahz Kumming*. Elmallah is the Anglified form of the Hebrew *el Mallakh*, which means "the angel" or "the messenger." Yet still I did not consider myself a religious person, nor did I imagine the poem would be religious in any sense. Hard to imagine I could write the following and yet not consider myself religious in some sense.

(Describing a pre-Sumerian encounter between the angel and Ertha):

He feels a vast surf washing up on the sand. It is Ertha's Conscience washed by his Knowledge and her perpetual forgetting. It is his energy penetrating her levels and withdrawing. It rushes – surf – he tells her of the Lord; withdraws – surf – she hears and recreates it in her Conscience. It rushes – surf – he sees how she has distorted his Knowledge; withdraws – surf – into his despair... The scene ends; for a moment Ertha glimpses a vision of the Lord – surf – is thunderstruck – surf – sees now the pantheon of Babylon standing above – surf – forgets that too – surf – remembers only that she has seen something awesome that she can't hold, can't comprehend.

The *Song ov Elmallahz Kumming* took about 13 years to write and I came out of it a very different person. The poem tells the story of tradition and history – very Jewish. G-d's presence in history is important for us to remember. G-d had provided me with a Jewish discernment process and it seemed natural to move back into my faith.

G-d still calls me to discernment most often through poetry. I remember that in 1996, when I was partially through the process of reconnecting with my faith tradition, I attended the bar mitzvah of the son of a man I considered a spiritual mentor. During the ceremony, poetry came streaming into my head.

It was so powerful that after the ceremony I ran home to write it down. It is called, *Among the ruins of the temple, I heard*. I wrote for hours and then returned in the evening for the celebration of this young man's religious initiation. As I rejoiced with him, I realized I was also rejoicing over my own spiritual awakening as a Jew.

BRIGID'S STORY

At the liturgy for my Silver Jubilee, 25 years as a Roman Catholic sister, I had a shocking fright, a gut feeling that hit with finality that I was to leave religious life. I had felt these uncomfortable, inner rumblings for a long time, without knowing the direction they were leading me. I knew this experience was of God, but I still ended up fighting it for ten years.

At first, I took a sabbatical. I went to Chicago and got another degree, a masters in pastoral studies (spirituality). All the new and wonderful things I had learned helped me to stifle the inner groanings. Shortly after returning home, though, I became depressed. I then tried a change of work. That didn't help and after a few years of this I was ready for another sabbatical.

Off I went to Chicago again for a doctor of ministry degree (spiritual direction). This time the depression didn't lift even though I loved my course of studies. So finally, I decided to practice what I had preached so often in my ministry of spiritual direction and teaching at universities and colleges.

I entered an intense process of self-exploration with a Jungian analyst, and spiritual direction with a no-nonsense Russian mystic. I also journaled extensively. I frequently taught journaling as discernment, using Ira Progoff's Intensive Journal process. I also had those who came to me for spiritual direction use a written clarification process as part of discerning their path.

I want to share the journaling process I used during this time. Prior to each session of journaling, I reminded myself to boldly tell the truth to myself, because the truth of my being is stronger than any thing, experience, idea, or belief. I always did an hour meditation before writing, using the mantra "Placing my life in your hands." This was to connect, center, and align myself to the divine within. I believe it is important to take time for this orienting to God. Then we really act in partnership.

Even at the beginning of my discernment process, I knew that the call was clear enough; my ego was stalling for time, trying to change God's mind. The process *did* clarify the blocks I was putting in the way of the call, which was very helpful. It is so easy for ego, rather than our true self, which is listening to God, to control the process. Because of this, for people interested in a journaling process for discernment, I suggest they learn a structured program such as Progoff's Intensive Journaling.

I journaled by putting my issue at the top of a page and then divided the page into four columns, like this:

Leaving my congregation

What is good about leaving	What is not so good about leaving	What is good about staying	What is not so good about staying

After my time of aligning with God in meditation, I prayerfully and honestly completed each column. Then I put the sheet away. Twice more I completed the process, never looking to see what I had already written. Doing it three times allows time for my repressed or unclear issues to present themselves and for God's message to get through. Pacing is important. Some people complete their sheet daily, others weekly.

After I completed my three sheets, I looked at the direction that had emerged to see if it was in line with scripture. I examined it in the light of this path leading to truth, freedom, life, peace, and joy. By this time I had done enough work on myself to realize that, although my time as a Catholic sister had been satisfying and had provided me with much healing, growth, and the opportunity to be of service, I had entered more for my own reasons than for God's.

I had entered religious life hoping to find the love and worthiness I did not feel within. I could see now that God was calling me to a different form of life. But what? As I sat pondering what to do, where to go, I said, "God, if this call is from you, give me a message!" A few moments later the phone rang. It was one of the secretaries from the Institute of Pastoral Studies in Chicago asking me to teach summer session. I was thrilled.

One thing led to another and I stayed in Chicago for six years. This was the transition time for me. I was still a religious, yet distanced from my community. I started to get a sense of what life would be like when I left. I am now 69; I left when I was 55. It was definitely the right decision. My self-esteem and self-image are greater now and I don't feel I have to wear a certain label or role to be loved by God and others.

SWAMI PADMANANDA'S STORY

I am a teacher of Swami Shivananda Radha's Kundalini Yoga for the West method. In this method you use the mind to go beyond the mind. We use self-investigation to discern the patterns within us that give us problems. Divine energy wants to flow strongly through us, guiding and enlightening. We need to help this process by cleaning up our senses. It is essential to have a spiritual practice where we can quiet the mind and then learn to let it go so that we can receive understanding from the Greater Divine through our own higher self.

I enter my discernment process by first clarifying, "What is this thing that is bothering me?" Then I put any thought of it aside and do my spiritual practice. Afterwards I keep quiet for some time. Then I write. Daily journaling is an important reflective process that allows submerged wisdom an outlet to come to the surface where we can use it.

I often journal by using an Ignatian journaling technique. I set a scene, pose my question, and then let the scene play out in my imagination. When I feel finished, I start writing whatever comes. I do not edit the flow of words. My issue or path may be clearer by the end of the writing, or it may take more time. I continue the process of spiritual practice and journaling, with trust and patience, until I have received the understanding from the Greater Divine that I am meant to have.

John English describes the Ignatian technique further.

> In Ignatian contemplation we form the habit of losing ourselves...in sacred events of great significance. After some initial practice, we learn how to stay with the scene and its actions, to relax in the presence of those who speak and move, and to open ourselves without reserve to what occurs, so that we may receive a deep impression of the event's mysterious meaning.[64]

If you feel interested in writing as a method of discernment, there are many workshops and books that teach various structured journaling processes. Some people prefer to use a blank notebook more informally and infrequently, recording inspirational quotes, God-touches, and other experiences of wonder.

Dreams

Sometimes dreams are wiser than waking.
BLACK ELK, LAKOTA HEALER

Are your dreams sent by God? Ultimately, only you can tell. And yet there are some signposts that can assist you. Many different faith traditions and cultures have recorded and interpreted dreams, viewing them as providing divine guidance and inspiration. Some, including the ancient Chinese, even had paid dream interpreters who held high positions in the government.

Dr. Kelly Bulkeley defines spiritual dreams as those "that reveal an aspect of the sacred, dreams that reveal something of the ultimate powers, truths and values of reality, however the dreamer conceptualizes them."[65] His book *Spiritual Dreaming* provides a history of spiritual dreams using examples from many cultures and religions. The book also describes a number of common themes and how they have been viewed and used.

It is rare for the literal meaning of a dream to be the true one. Dreams speak to us in the rich language of metaphor. They are frequently explored through journaling, talking to another who has experience in working with dreams, becoming a member of a dream group, or simply going about life, trusting that God will send a message of clarification in some other manner.

People who experience dreams they believe to be divinely inspired often say there is a flavor or image from the dream that lingers, even while they are on about their day. Or they know it's God-sent because they wake with a feeling of awe, gratitude, love, or joy. When they apply the principles outlined in the previous section, "How do I know it's God?" the dream fits the criteria.

Some people remember dreams nightly; others are not aware of ever dreaming. Most view their dreams as experiences that cannot be influenced. Some dream researchers and authors have explored the phenomenon called *lucid* dreaming. This occurs when sleepers know they are dreaming. Sometimes they are able to act in ways that influence the dream, for example, asking questions of a wise being or deciding to travel to a certain destination.

Bulkeley, in his chapter on lucid dreaming, states that "the spiritual impact of these dreams comes not from any specific content, but rather from the extraordinary power of vision that people gain: lucid dreams enable the dreamers to perceive important new aspects of reality, and thus to transform ordinary waking consciousness." (Bulkeley, p. 77) Dr. Stephen LaBerge is a dream researcher. His books on lucid dreaming (*Lucid Dreaming* and *Exploring the World of Lucid Dreaming*) teach a process to dream in this manner. Examples of lucid spiritual dreams can be found in the books mentioned above.

In this section, I have included dreams that sleepers believed were sent by the divine to guide them on their path. We begin with an example from Genesis in the Hebrew scriptures. Joseph, son of Jacob and Rachel, used dreams as a discernment method.

JOSEPH'S STORY

Joseph was Jacob's favorite son. His brothers were already jealous of him, when, as a teenager, he eagerly and not too tactfully told them the following dream.

> He said to them, "Listen to this dream that I dreamed. There we were, binding sheaves in the field. Suddenly my sheaf rose and stood upright; then your sheaves gathered around it and bowed down to my sheaf. His brothers said to him, 'Are you indeed to reign over us? Are you indeed to have dominion over us?' So they hated him even more because of his dreams and his words" (Genesis 37:6–8).

Joseph's brothers sold him into slavery and hid their crime by telling Jacob that a wild animal had killed him. During his slavery, Joseph became known as an accurate dream interpreter. His fortunes rose dramatically when the Pharaoh of Egypt had two disturbing dreams.

> Pharaoh dreamed that he was standing by the Nile, and there came up out of the Nile seven sleek and fat cows, and they grazed in the reed grass. Then seven other cows, ugly and thin came up out of the Nile after them, and stood by the other cows on the bank of the Nile. The ugly and thin cows ate up the seven sleek and fat cows. And Pharaoh awoke. Then he fell asleep and dreamed a second time; seven ears of grain, plump and good, were growing on one stalk. Then seven ears, thin and blighted by the east wind, sprouted after them. The thin ears swallowed up the seven plump and full ears. Pharaoh awoke, and it was a dream. In the morning his spirit was troubled; so he sent and called for all the magicians of Egypt and all its wise men. Pha-

raoh told them his dreams but there was no one who could interpret them to Pharaoh (Genesis 41:1–8).

Then Pharaoh's cupbearer remembered how Joseph had helped him.
When Joseph was brought before the ruler and asked for his advice, he
answered, "It is not I; God will give Pharaoh a favorable answer" (Genesis
41:16). Upon hearing the dreams, Joseph interpreted them as meaning
God was warning of a seven-year famine that was to strike the land of
Egypt after seven years of plenty. Pharaoh was being given an opportunity
to prepare for this future.

Pharaoh believed this interpretation and was grateful for the warning.
Joseph, having learned some tact during his years of slavery, did not
directly ask for a reward. His statement, "Now therefore let Pharaoh select
a man who is discerning and wise, and set him over the land of Egypt"
(Genesis 41:33), did not go unheeded, though. Joseph got the job.

MY STORY

These four dreams came over a four-day period. I will describe the issue,
recount the dreams, and give some information of the "flow" of the four
days. This material is taken from my journal, with additions when expla-
nation seems useful. I've also included the other ways God helped me
clarify and find a way through this issue.

Day 1: Wonderful day, helped at church bazaar in morning, massage and
spiritual companioning session in afternoon. On way to the library afterwards, thought, "Life is heaven." At that moment, a still, quiet but firm
voice inside me says, "Now it's time to work on vengeance." I'm shocked
and very resistant. "Vengeance is not a very big issue with me," I respond
defensively. In answer, I see the image of a woman being "a little bit preg-
nant." "Look," I say as reasonably as I can, "I'm feeling really happy and
content with my life; I'll work on vengeance later. It would only be an
issue if someone murdered my daughter or something." No response and
I thought I'd won.

In the library, I look for a light, romantic book about a saint. I don't
know much about saints and have recently had the thought it would be

fun to read more about them. A small book catches my eye: *The Way of St. Francis*, by Murray Bodo. The only things I associate with Francis are love of animals and nature, the romantic movie *Brother Sun, Sister Moon*, and garden statues. Just the book to take my mind off vengeance, I think, and still show God I'm interested in developing spiritually.

That night I have the following dream.

Day 1 dream: I and two companions are walking to a new country where we are going to live. Feeling of eager anticipation. We encounter three large beautiful wolves sitting in the road, barring our way. We know we can't escape them, so I tell my companions I'll try to tame them. (I do some dog training in my waking life.) I tell the wolves to "Lie down! Sit!" and then "Heel!" The wolves obediently come with us, but the feeling grows that they are not really under my control; they are only choosing for this time to heed me.

We become increasingly nervous and when the large home we "know" will be ours comes into view, we run in quickly and lock the door to keep the wolves out. Time passes and I begin to feel restricted, even though the house is large and beautiful. I want to go out into the new country I can see from the windows, but am afraid of the wolves.

Finally, I tell my companions that I haven't seen the wolves for a while and maybe they have gone. I unlock the door and open it a crack, confident that I can close it quickly if needed. The biggest wolf has been waiting for that opening and pushes in. He sits in front of me, his head on the level of mine, and we look at each other for a few moments. Then he explains to me telepathically that I/we are too dangerous to other creatures as we are. Our capacity to injure or kill is too great. The only solution is for him to eat our right hands. I am free to refuse, but would then not be allowed access to the wonderful country.

I let him eat my right hand, which hurts, bleeds, then heals very quickly. Now I'm free in the new country. One of my companions refuses and stays in the house. Time passes and I look at a photograph of many people, all without right hands. The new country is filling up well. Then a friend tells me that the companion who refused to give his right hand has tried to kill the wolf and it had to eat him…

I wake at 3 a.m. feeling calm and as I remember and write the dream in my journal, the realization grows of how dangerous vengeance is. I vow to God that I will work in partnership to let it go. Feeling pleased with myself, I turn the light off and think I'll get a few more hours sleep.

Ten minutes later, I'm having a panic attack: heart racing, difficulty breathing, wanting to run. The implications of what I have vowed are starting to sink in. I remember how often I "get back" at people who have done something I don't like, such as trying to make them feel guilty for what they have done. I think of how judgmental I am in sneaky ways, letting others know that someone else has "hurt" me. The thought of letting these "protections" go now brings great anxiety.

No more sleep for me. I start fighting God. I try rationalizations: "I'm only human," "I need some protection and this way is not as harmful as some," "We can't all be like Jesus." I try to get God mad at me so I have a "legitimate" reason to withdraw. I cry. I sulk. That day, I find all my clients irritate me and it takes a great deal of energy to act caring.

My workday ends early, at 3 p.m., and I immediately lie down for a nap. I'm exhausted! It's very hard to keep a one-sided fight going. I have a strong sense that God is loving me throughout this time, which at first makes me even angrier. Now there is a strong bereft feeling, knowing I have intentionally stepped away from God. I don't know how this issue can be resolved but I ask for help. "Where do I start?"

Into my mind comes The Lord's Prayer. Okay, I can say that. I confidently start, but get stuck on the first word – "Our." "Our" means everyone. It means letting go of vengeful feelings towards everyone. It takes me half an hour to get through the whole prayer, as I really listen to and say "yes" to all the words. I then fall asleep and dream.

Dream 2: I and a number of other people are going to participate in a dog agility competition. (I do this in "real life.") I get the idea it would be wonderful to provide the others with a banquet before the trial. I go to a lot of work to arrange a large breakfast, but nobody comes. I then realize that no one wants to come to a breakfast before a competition; they are all too busy preparing.

As I wake with this dream filling my consciousness, I think of the phrase, "Not my will, but Thine be done." My ego will have lots of good ideas of what to put in the place of vengeance. I will need to listen to what God wants me to do.

That night I have the following dream.

Dream 3: (Only remember a snippet.) There are a number of circles on the ground and I am helping someone walk from one to the other. I say, "You have to paint yourself into a corner and then get out for it to work."

I want this issue resolved. It's hard to be patient. I've been reading my St. Francis book. Interestingly, a lot of it is about Francis' struggle with vengeance. One sentence hits hard: "For Francis peace is inseparable from peace of soul, and neither can be achieved without the risk of loving your supposed or real enemies."[66] Oh, no! Not only let go of vengeance, but love those I feel hurt by. Trying to decide myself how far I should take this, I decide to go to a evening worship service. The sermon turns out to be about the importance and difficulty of loving those we see doing injustice!

Okay, Okay. I get the point. That night, in bed, I take time to hold the image of many people in my life I have felt anger or vengeful towards. Hard to do. Still not feeling clear on how God wants me to be since I feel threatened at the thought of letting go my vengeance "shield." I remember a phrase I coined a few years ago: "Vengeance is the most seductive drug we have," because it gives the illusion of power and strength.

I fall asleep and dream.

Dream 4: My husband, Bob, and I are walking in a strange desert country to bring precious treaties/agreements to the king. Entering the king's town, powerful people who are against the king try to capture us. Bob and I realize we have to separate and run. Some passersby help us escape.

Then I find myself lying in a small cloth tent. A woman is with me. She is standing where others can see her and accepting food for me from other women. They can see me peeking out of the tent, but the enemy, who is roaring around on horses looking for me, can't. I know Bob has been found by some wise men and is safe.

I finally work up enough courage to enter the palace courtyard. I am feeling very vulnerable. Some men greet me and say they want to help me. One shows me a large chart on the wall and suggests the information will assist me. Then, as I start to read, he leans forward and begins to rub himself against me in sexual invitation. I realize that one way to protect myself from the enemy is to align myself with this man's power. Another is through information. I sense these are not appropriate ways for me and tell him so. He accepts this and immediately moves away from me.

Then he says he can teach me martial arts to protect me. I try a few moves with him, but realize although I can learn them, this is not the way to go either. I look around at the men trying to help me and say, "The king will protect me if I just make myself visible enough." They respond that I might get hurt before the king arrives. I acknowledge the truth of this and tell them that's all right; I know the king will find me.

I awaken, peaceful and resolved. That day I feel very compassionate with my clients. Two days later, I receive a telephone call from an agency with which my clinic has a contract. A young person's body has just been discovered and another young person has been charged with manslaughter. I am asked to provide crisis counseling for the adults and children who knew the two personally or professionally.

Although I have done this type of counseling before, I had used anger about the injustice as a shield to protect myself from the deep pain I felt and experienced in others. I hid the anger deep inside as I helped others work through their trauma. At the end of each day I would feel exhausted and "polluted" and the gulf between the pain and my home life seemed huge. I then needed many self-care strategies to release the hurtful feelings.

This time, I went into the crisis sessions without anger. I felt much more vulnerable, although I quickly found that the emotional pain was slowly being absorbed by my feeling of compassion. At the end of each day, I came home feeling much "cleaner" inside and I was able to enter emotionally into my home life without difficulty. The individuals and groups I worked with initially expressed a great deal of anger, blame and anxiety, and spoke frequently of getting revenge. I noticed a quicker shift than usual to expressions of compassion and sadness.

Through the dreams and daytime struggles, I allowed God to transform my "protection" from anger and vengefulness to compassion and peacefulness. At times I still experience vengeful feelings, yet am able to be aware of them quicker and feel more deeply the importance of allowing them to change.

DENISE'S STORY

For 20 years I had a recurring dream. In the dream, I would walk into a new house I had just purchased. Each time it was a different house, yet the dream unfolded in the same way. I enjoyed looking through each room until I came to a particular closed door. I just knew there was evil behind that door! At that point, I would wake in a cold sweat.

Then, one night, my dream was of the house I was actually living in at the time. In it, I was looking for a space for myself. There seemed to be no room for me. My husband's things, including many old "dead" files, took up all the space. Again I encountered the closed door where evil dwelled. This time I opened the door, walked in and screamed, "Get out! This is my space!" The evil fled and a golden light appeared.

The Goddess was telling me something, but what? A week later, I discovered my husband was having an affair. Our marriage had been unhappy for many years. The dream gave me the direction I needed. This was the moment for change. I turfed him. It was interesting that shortly after that my allergies cleared up.

As a Wiccan chaplain, I take signs from the divine very seriously. Often, a sign like my recurring dream will grab my attention, creating a mindset that won't let me go. I wait and trust, knowing that the answer is already within me. At some point, when the answer is needed, it will surface, and I can act upon it.

There are many techniques to explore dreams. Spiritual directors, counselors, workshops, and courses are all available to assist the person who feels led deeper into their dream experiences.

Retreats

But in the grey of the morning
My mind becomes confused
Between the dead and the sleeping
and the road that I must choose.
I'm looking for someone to change my life
I'm looking for a miracle in my life.
JUSTIN HAYWARD[67]

Until recently, it has been a common perception that retreats were for clergy, other religious, and maybe for "religious fanatics." Yet a time of withdrawal from the world, a time of rest and renewal, a time to be more present to the Source of all our Being, is a need periodically felt by most people.

My grieving clients frequently express the desire to get away either for a break from the concerns and duties in their day-to-day lives, or to open more fully to their healing process. The thought of staying in a resort or hotel may not give the image of peace and nurture they are wanting. Similarly, staying with friends or family may meet some needs and desires, yet not provide the quiet they crave.

Retreat centers come in an incredible variety of sizes and types. With a bit of research, it is possible to find a center that can meet even unusual needs. Most faith traditions have some type of "get away" place and most welcome retreatants of other faiths or denominations. There are tiny one-person hermitages on the grounds of a monastery and large centers where a number of workshops or structured retreat programs are always occurring.

Some retreat centers offer spiritual direction; some expect that retreatants take part in some worship or housekeeping activities. Meals are included in some centers; at others, the retreatant is expected to bring food and/or to provide their own meals. A retreatant may be attracted to a center where days are spent in silence; at other times, a boisterous church camp involving people of all ages in a variety of programs, may be what's needed.

Some people are attracted to the idea of a retreat to help with their discernment process. If you are feeling such a desire, it helps to clarify what type of retreat would be most appropriate. Unless you are very experienced in the art of discernment, a spiritual director or companion can be invaluable at helping clarify and support you on your path. Check to see if the center you are thinking of attending provides direction and that a director is available to you during your time there. Sometimes the demand exceeds the resources.

An individual, directed retreat appeals to some. For others, a structured retreat or workshop offers a focus in which your individual concern can be structured. If you are trying to answer a call to live a more simple lifestyle, for example, a retreat on voluntary simplicity may give you suggestions and bring you into contact with others who hear a similar call. Prior to booking a workshop or structured retreat, it can be useful to read something written by the facilitator of a retreat or to talk to others who have had contact with that person to determine whether you resonate with their message.

Queenswood, our local retreat center, offers theme retreats that focus on the church year and that range from an evening to a week or longer. Some of their recent offerings include "Spiritspace Gathering of Women," "Mid-Life Directions," "Ecofeminism," "Growing Together as a Couple," "The Labyrinth," and a "Retreat Day with Mary."

ROSE'S STORY

I am accustomed to making a retreat each year in the silence and solitude of a hermitage. Since lately I had been pondering the question of aging, with the subsequent diminishing energy, I realized that it may be time to make a decision as to whether I should move to a care facility. The focus for this latest retreat, then, was on making this decision.

Within the first day or two, as I was settling into the silence, prayer centered around the acceptance of aging. In spirit, I knew that the whole process was part of nature, and I couldn't buck it. Spending time with the issue in prayer allowed me to reach a place of surrender around it.

I then settled into dealing with the *decision* of whether to move or not. I drew up a list of pros and cons of staying or leaving, going to a care home or not. For the next two or three days, with prayerful reflection, I wrote down thoughts, feelings, and *reasons* under one column or another. When I had written all that I could, it seemed evident that the sensible thing would be to move.

Making a *tentative decision* to do so, I then set the whole thing aside to deal with when I returned home. I turned my heart and mind to centering prayer and meditation. The result was unexpected. A sense of restlessness and dissatisfaction that I could not understand grew in me over the next two days. In praying about this, I realized I was in discernment and that the tentative decision to move was not God's will for me at this time.

With this realization came a deep sense of gratitude that the movement of the Spirit of God is so active in my life. I will be told if I start down the wrong path. Now that I knew God's will, the only response was a "yes." I knew this involved staying in my apartment taking my aging into consideration. I would need to reach out more and accept more offers of practical help from my friends.

The issue now felt resolved. As confirmation of this, the rest of my stay in the hermitage flowed in a wonderful peace, in full awareness of nature around me and God's Spirit within.

IGNATIAN DISCERNMENT

We have already met Ignatius of Loyola as he was discerning his call to follow Jesus Christ rather than to seek the world's definition of fame and fortune. Ignatius placed much emphasis on individual and group discernment, taking a great deal of time to clarify God's will for the Society of Jesus.

John English says Ignatius emphasized "a spirituality of discernment, that is, the ability to recognize the presence of God and diverse spirits in culture, as they are experienced interiorly, and the ability to know the significance of these interior movements for carrying on the work of Christ in the world."[68]

Ignatius developed a highly structured 30-day retreat, which he called the "Spiritual Exercises." English states, "Persons make the Exercises to find meaning and self-realization, deepen their relationship with God, discover God's desires for them, and make decisions about their lives." (p. 239) "A basic goal of the Exercises is to awaken in us a freedom to choose according to the spirits or motivations underlying our possible choices." (p. 243)

The Exercises consist of a number of spiritual practices that help people to a deeper encounter with Jesus Christ, through various times in their life. Daily spiritual direction is also part of the experience. Some retreat centers offer the Exercises as a weekly program over a number of months, for those who would not be able to undertake the month-long format.

KATE FAGAN'S STORY

I'm 30 years old and in a time of flux. I've been in the helping profession for a number of years and was trying to decide whether to continue as I have been, or to change my career path. As a Catholic, the year 2000, the year of Jubilee, really spoke to me. Jubilee is a specified time when people and the earth go through a period of renewal by lying fallow. In my very busy life, the thought of rest and renewal sounded wonderful, yet I wasn't sure how to accomplish it.

One day, a friend "lit the spark" by mentioning the Ignatian Spiritual Exercises. He talked about the Guelph, Ontario, program, which lasted 40 days. I immediately saw myself lying fallow for those 40 days, deepening my prayer life and exploring my questions with God. Since their program coincided with my summer holidays, I was able to apply for one that started a few months later.

My director helped me to clarify and explore my questions. We examined the attachments that keep me from being free to be the person I am meant to be. He helped me see that my deepest desires are also God's will for me. Praying five hours a day and meeting daily with my director brought a deepening of my relationship with God.

I was having difficulty with my decisions, however. I was journaling advantages and disadvantages, and praying through the various contemplations. And I wasn't receiving a confirmation for the path that I thought would be best for me. I asked my director how I would know when I received confirmation. Maybe I was missing it. He said, "You'll know. It will be obvious."

I kept praying for one path. I wanted a decision. The word that kept coming to me in prayer, however, was "Wait." Waiting is hard for me. As I waited, I looked more closely at the advantages and disadvantages I had written and realized that I had interpreted them based on what I thought was the best path for me. I was trying to push for a certain outcome because I wasn't as keen on the other path.

Finally, I was willing to pray for the other path. I received an avalanche of confirmation, including a great sense of freedom. What a surprise! By the time I left the retreat, I was clear on my general direction.

I still have to clarify timing and the specifics of my path. I'm more willing, though, to wait for God's unfolding of these aspects of the journey. I am very glad I made the retreat. The Spiritual Exercises provided a structured renewal time where I could rest with and in God, and also work on putting my ego aside so I could open to and follow my deepest desires.

An attitude of receptivity and patience will help you benefit from your retreat. Your concern may not be clear or resolved by the end of the experience. You may even find that you received direction about an issue that you had not consciously brought to the retreat. I have sometimes made a retreat with an issue burning in my heart, only to find that trying to explore it felt like hitting a brick wall. When I questioned this, I received images of resting, eating, sleeping, walking in the woods. If I was able to follow these suggestions, I returned from my retreat refreshed. Sometime later, I received clarity around my discernment issue. We have a choice of working on our time, or God's time.

To find a retreat center in your area, contact the administration center of the various faith communities in your region, or use the resources listed in "Suggested Reading" at the end of this book.

Walking

We have only to follow the thread of the hero path,
and where we had thought to find an abomination, we shall find a god.
And where we had thought to slay another, we shall slay ourselves.
Where we had thought to travel outward,
we will come to the center of our own existence.
And where we had thought to be alone, we will be with all the world.
JOSEPH CAMPBELL[69]

Many faith traditions have spiritual practices that involve the body. Some, Hatha Yoga for instance, are a central part of the tradition. This section includes stories about walking to discernment. The walk may take us to a different geographical area, such as on a pilgrimage or a walkabout, or we may travel a short distance, walking a labyrinth or making a vision quest. Sometimes a geographical destination is known. At other times, we may follow Spirit's leading into the unknown. The peregrination, for example, was a Celtic spiritual practice that involved setting out to sea in a rudderless coracle.

LABYRINTH

Dr. Lauren Artress is an Episcopalian priest and canon at Grace Cathedral in San Francisco. She is well known for her interest in the ancient spiritual tool called the labyrinth. Thousands of people from all spiritual paths have attended her lectures, retreats and/or read her book *Walking a Sacred Path: Rediscovering the Labyrinth as a Spiritual Tool*. In her book, she explains that types of labyrinths can be found in many spiritual traditions. Labyrinths can be found in Christian cathedrals in Europe, the most famous being the one at Chartres, France. The Jewish mystical tradition has the *Kabbala* or Tree of Life. Then there is the North American Hopi medicine wheel and Tibetan sand paintings.

Artress says, "The labyrinth is a spiritual tool meant to waken us to the deep rhythm that unites us to ourselves and to the Light that calls from within."[70] Unlike a maze which tries to trick us and keep us from the center by the use of dead ends and enticing side paths, the labyrinth has only one path for both the inward and outward journey.

Imagine a circular form with a winding path leading to a small centered clearing. By disregarding the path, we could reach the center in a few steps. Staying on the path means walking approximately one third of a mile in some labyrinths. Unless we view "journey" as necessary for our spiritual healing and growth, we would walk directly to the "goal."

So, for many, the labyrinth is a metaphor for their spiritual lives. Walking it can encourage a more intentional connection with the divine, with self, with others, and with the world. Artress includes a number of stories in her book from those who discovered self-awareness, healing, transformation, balance, grounding, and discernment in their walk. She says there are many ways Spirit can guide us. Not as well known but equally valid is the guidance that "comes through forms, patterns and symbols that impart sacred meaning." (Artress, p. 13)

It has been my experience that every labyrinth and every labyrinth walk is different. Spirit works with who we are right now. If I ask about a certain issue in my life yet another one is actually bubbling more strongly in me, the second is the one that will be brought into clearer focus. Rather than asking a yes or no question, walking with an open-ended receptivity discourages ego and allows us to hear more clearly. Also, it may be that some healing is necessary prior to discernment. If we look for what we have been given through the labyrinth rather than what we expected to get, some of our present needs will be met.

There are many ways to walk the labyrinth: fast, slow, dancing, silent, chanting, singing, stopping at intervals, etc. Being as present to self as possible leads us to the mode of moving that is most helpful for us at any given time.

There is probably a labyrinth in your community or at least within a few hours drive. My city of Victoria, British Columbia, has four outdoor public labyrinths: one is painted on the parking lot of a United church; another is in a city-owned park; there is one at Queenswood retreat center, and another beside the Anglican cathedral. There is even one private labyrinth painted on the turnaround of a paved driveway. Some people use their finger to "walk" through small painted or carved labyrinths.

PETER'S STORY

I work as an employee at the post office to receive the financial resources that support my passions: being a grandfather, spiritual director, and softball player. I believe that God has a project for me and my journey is to find out what it is. The stereotypical type of prayer I was taught as a child is not conducive to a felt connection with the divine. Neither does it answer questions about my path.

At first, I tried to live other peoples' paths and thought the more difficult they were, the better they must be. Finally, with God's assistance I found my own path, which is outside of organized religion. Communing with God in nature is a very profound experience for me.

During discernment, the Creator affirms a particular way by providing an Aha! in my head, a Spirit-driven insight, an increase in perspective about an issue or question. I sometimes experience, for a split second, the sense of a supportive person at my side, or an emotional warmth within.

A few years ago, I was part of a team directing a ten-day silent retreat. One of the retreatants telephoned a few weeks prior to the experience and told me about a new spiritual tool. She asked if she could construct a labyrinth for use during the retreat. It was the first time I had heard of a labyrinth and I was hesitant. I did not want to encourage a tool that might compartmentalize and limit an experience of Mystery. So I said no to the retreatant because I had no personal experience with a labyrinth.

About a month later, Victoria's first labyrinth was constructed in a church parking lot. I was one of the first to walk it. If I received a similar request, I wanted to decide based on personal experience.

For the last few years, since that first experience, I have walked the labyrinth most mornings at 7 a.m. For me, it is like going out to meet God. I always walk the path with an attitude of gratitude; my only desire is to be present to the divine. I then find it easier to let go of ego and allow my heart to be engaged as well as my brain. Using my body to pray is another important aspect, giving the sense that I am bringing my all to the All.

The shape of the labyrinth is a mirror of my life. In 30 seconds I'm almost to the center. Then, as I continue to walk, I move away from it for a while. I don't ask a question as I begin the walk. I trust that the Holy Spirit will give me the insights and direction for a particular problem or issue.

Over the years, this has happened many times. I find it interesting that I always receive a message as I am walking into the center, never *at* the center or on the outward journey. Recently, I experienced a major stress in my life and began to respond to it in familiar ways. Soon after, I entered the labyrinth, only to find a mom, dad, and small child running the outward path. As each exited they shouted, "I'm out! I'm out!" Hearing these cries, I experienced my Spirit Aha! and knew it was time to let a disowned part of myself out of the container I had created for it. I could see in that moment how limited my response to this stress would be if I did not become friends with this repressed aspect.

PILGRIMAGE – THE DALAI LAMA'S STORY
In a foreword to Courtney Milne's book of stunning photographs called *The Sacred Earth*, The Dalai Lama writes the following.

Throughout history people all over the world have identified particular places as sacred, some because of their association with a sacred event, and others due to uplifting qualities intrinsic to the places themselves. Closely connected with this is the practice of pilgrimage…I remember being profoundly moved myself when as a young man I first visited the Buddhist holy places in India. It gave me a very special inspiration to think that at this or that place the Buddha himself had meditated and taught. Somehow I felt more closely connected to him and his teaching as a result. Similarly, when I visited Assisi I felt privileged to have joined the throngs of pilgrims who had come there over the centuries, attracted by the ideal of kindheartedness embodied by St. Francis.[71]

Although the word pilgrimage usually evokes thoughts of travel to exotic or at least distant places, even a trip to the store for groceries can be undertaken as a pilgrimage, with the right attitude. It helps to be as present as possible, to be aware of the reality that everything around us is sacred, and to let go of our preconceptions of how God will speak to us. Whenever we notice that we are thinking of the past or future, we can gently return our awareness to the present.

Since it may be easier at first to see the sacred at a holy site rather that in the dairy section of the local store, most people choose the former as a pilgrimage destination. Such a trip usually involves much planning and the availability of time, energy, and financial resources. Every part of the pilgrimage, from the first thought to washing your clothes upon your return, may give you guidance, if you allow it.

Phil Cousineau, author of *The Art of Pilgrimage*, speaks of it as "a powerful metaphor for any journey with the purpose of finding something that matters deeply to the traveler."[72] He speaks of seven phases of any pilgrimage: The Longing, The Call, Departure, The Pilgrim's Way, The Labyrinth, Arrival, and Bringing Back the Boon.

SHANTI'S STORY

I had just come through a time of many large life changes. When I asked for guidance around the new life I was about to undertake, I heard a call to pilgrimage. I didn't know what that would mean, but I trusted the guidance that this was what I needed. I moved into this unknown in a "faith-full" way. As I prayed about it, certain aspects of the journey became clearer. Part of the discernment was to journey to a number of sacred places throughout the world. I would keep the following three desires/goals in mind:

1. I would conduct a ceremony of thanksgiving at each sacred site.
2. I would experience and deepen my understanding of various cultures. This would enhance my engagement in my multicul tural working environment.
3. I would celebrate the freedom of my new life by traveling to unknown destinations.

Planning for the pilgrimage involved researching, talking to former travelers, and praying to be led to the places that would be most closely aligned with the emerging purpose of the journey. My experience at this particular point was a total trusting of my inner guidance that the path would unfold. I have many stories of divine intervention on this journey. I'm going to share this one because it demonstrated to me the importance of being receptive and flexible to the deeper nuances of the call. What may look like a dead end can be a springboard to a new direction.

The story began when I entered Jerusalem. I had planned to stay at a hostel in the country, but after telephoning found there was "no room at the inn." I really wanted to stay in this hostel and when the receptionist suggested another, I told her a number of times that I didn't want to go there. Finally, it sunk in that my plans would have to be changed and I reluctantly made the neces-sary arrangements.

The hostel that could take me was a Roman Catholic one in the Old Quarter of Jerusalem. In my small, clean room, I listened to the hustle and bustle of the busy street outside and decided to retire shortly. An early start would give more time to find the holy sites of the city.

Lying in bed, I suddenly became aware of a presence in the room. I had never experienced anything like it before and was quite unnerved. The energy seemed concentrated in a corner of my bedroom and as I focused on it, I saw a vague white light. Awestruck, I heard a deep inner voice say, "Do not be afraid," and I experienced a peace transcending normal peace.

I knew I was experiencing something of a divine nature. After a few moments, the presence faded away. As it left, I began to cry in a deep primal way. I didn't understand this profound womb-crying. I sobbed for a long time and gradually became aware that I was weeping with sadness for the pain and suffering of the world. Eventually, I fell asleep, giving thanks for the visitation.

The next morning, the experience was still very much with me. Feeling full of love and gratitude, I was even more eager to experience the holy sites of the city. I asked one of the nuns at breakfast for directions. The woman suggested I start in the basement of the hostel. But this place wasn't mentioned in the research I had done. When I asked what was in the basement, the nun just smiled.

Visiting hours for tourists had not begun, so I found myself alone as I descended to the basement and then down more stairs to ancient stone paving. Approaching a roped off area with explanatory signs in various languages, I realized that I was standing almost directly below my bedroom. After reading the sign, I experienced a need to be directly below where I thought the presence had been.

Slipping under the ropes, I walked to the spot and again felt that overwhelming grief for the pain and suffering of the world. The sign I had read explained that this was the Lithostrotos, the place where Pontius Pilate had condemned Jesus of Nazareth to death and then had tried to deny responsibility by washing his hands.

For me, this felt like a mystical experience of being guided to encounter the presence of Christ. This grace has deepened my relationship with the Holy.

PEACE PILGRIM'S STORY

"A pilgrimage can be to a place – that's the best-known kind – but it can also be for a thing. Mine is for peace, and that is why I am a Peace Pilgrim."[73] We never knew her name (she called herself Peace Pilgrim) or her birth date or place of birth. All of that was irrelevant she said. Only her message of peace mattered.

For 28 years, from January 1, 1953, to 1981, she walked across the United States, including Alaska and Hawaii; Canada; and parts of Mexico. She asked for nothing. When she was offered food, she ate; when she was offered a bed, she slept in it. Otherwise, she went hungry and slept on the ground. She said that she had no religious upbringing and did not subscribe to a particular religion.

Her spirituality shone clearly in her. "What I walk on is not the energy of youth, it is a better energy. I walk on the endless energy of inner peace that never runs out! When you become a channel through which God works there are no more limitations, because God does the work through you: you are merely the instrument – and what God can do is unlimited." (Peace Pilgrim, p. 26)

Peace Pilgrim spoke of her long intentional spiritual growth. She knew God was encouraging and challenging her to let go of ego and to cherish her true self. She had always felt an urge to be of service and had worked for many years with mentally and emotionally wounded people, and with organizations promoting peace.

One morning, she felt a deep alignment with God and knew she had reached a place in her spiritual growth where her receptivity to the will of God could be relied on.

> I went out for a time alone with God. While I was out a thought struck my mind: I felt a strong inner motivation toward the pilgrimage – toward this special way of witnessing for peace. I saw, in my mind's eye, myself walking along and wearing the garb of my mission…I saw a map of the United States with the large cities marked – and it was as though someone had taken a colored crayon and marked a zigzag line across, coast to coast and border to border, from Los Angeles to New York City. I knew what I was to do. And that was a vision of my first year's pilgrimage route in 1953! (Peace Pilgrim, p. 22)

> With the last bit of money I had left, I bought not only paper and stencil for my first messages but material for my first tunic. Although I designed it, the sewing was done by a lady in California,

and the lettering was painted by a man who was a sign painter My initial reaction when I first put it on was a wonderful "rightness" about it, and I immediately accepted it. (Peace Pilgrim, p. 24)

Peace Pilgrim walked through the deeply judgmental times of the McCarthy era, through the times of the Korean and Vietnam wars, through the pain and struggle of the birthings of racial equality. She approached no one with her message. She just walked, wearing her tunic, with only a toothbrush, comb, and writing materials in her pockets. If someone spoke to her, she willingly answered their questions.

Her message was the same throughout the years. "This is the way of peace – overcome evil with good, and falsehood with truth, and hatred with love." (Peace Pilgrim, p. 26) To this basic message, she periodically gathered names for petitions, such as the one pleading for an immediate peace in Korea. She was asked to speak in many churches and other public meetings throughout her pilgrimage. Peace Pilgrim was killed instantly in a head-on collision as she was being driven to speak to a public gathering in Indiana, on July 7, 1981. A group of her friends gathered her words and published them in the book *Peace Pilgrim*.

MATSUO BASHO'S STORY

The Japanese poet Basho (1644–1694) is renowned for his haiku, the elegantly simple poetry form which expresses volumes in a few lines. Basho's poetry reflected his Zen Buddhist spirituality. He wrote much of it on long pilgrimages to shrines, temples, and places of natural beauty. Basho may be one of the originators of the bumper sticker. He wrote signs which he wore on his pilgrim's hat: "Homeless I wander, in company with God," "Soon, cherry blossoms," "With the Buddha."

In his book *Narrow Road to the Interior*, Basho speaks simultaneously of a pilgrimage into the center of Japan and into the center of the soul. He discerned where to travel next by being as present as possible to his surroundings and by responding to inner and outer signs that enthused him. This might be another traveler met by happenstance who told him of an interesting twisted pine, or hearing that a celebration was to take place at a nearby temple.

His travel journals include his haiku, poetry of others he met along the way, and a description of the people and places he visited. I've included an excerpt to give the flavor of his writing.

In Yamagata Province, the ancient temple founded by Jikaku Daishi, in 860, Ryushaku Temple, is stone quiet, perfectly tidy. Everyone told us to see it. It meant a few miles extra, doubling back toward Obanazawa to find shelter. Monks at the foot of the mountain offered rooms, then we climbed the ridge to the temple, scrambling up through ancient gnarled pine and oak, smooth gray stones and moss. The temple doors, built on rocks, were bolted. I crawled among boulders to make my bows at shrines. The silence was profound. I sat, feeling my heart begin to open.

Lonely silence
a single cicada's cry
sinking into stone[74]

As these stories show, there are many ways to use movement to open more fully to an awareness of the divine. The people who talked to me about these methods stressed the importance of stepping into the unknown. If we are looking for the holy to manifest in a certain way or to give us guidance about a particular issue, we will most likely hear a message from our ego.

WWJ (et. al.) D?

An arouser of faith appears in the world.
One associates oneself with such a person.
THE BUDDHA[75]

Some years ago in a Christian oriented bookstore, I came across a large display stand of woven, rainbow colored bracelets carrying in large print the initials WWJD? "What does your bracelet mean?" I asked the young sales clerk. She beamed, "It stands for 'What Would Jesus Do?' See mine? It allows me to witness to my faith when someone questions me and I try to ask myself that question, especially when I'm mad at someone. I remember that Jesus would show compassion and forgiveness and I try to do that. If I'm not too mad." Since that first encounter with WWJD?, I have found it on bumper stickers, buttons, T-shirts, and posters.

The Concise Oxford Dictionary defines "charisma" as "Divinely conferred power or talent; capacity to inspire followers with devotion or enthusiasm." The associated term "charism" is widely used in Christian religious orders and societies to denote the special gift or particular grace of God associated with their founders or other people seen as living surrendered to the divine.

A number of people may have the charism of healing. Taking their other gifts into consideration, one might be led to found and run a hospital in a remote rural area without medical care; another might work on the streets in a large city. Although every person has been given many gifts, one often stands out as almost defining that person or their ministry. It is difficult to think of Gandhi without also thinking of non-violence.

The charism "flavors" the religious group, and individuals are often attracted to join because they resonate with that quality. It may be a gift they feel strongly within themselves, or one they want to nurture. Vatican II gave a radical challenge to Roman Catholic groups to be more aligned to the charism of their founder. A number of these groups had become extremely diverse in their ministries and Pope John XXIII was concerned that their particular gift would be diluted. So communities made necessary changes to live their original charism more fully.

I believe we all have a charism. Nurturing this gift helps us grow into the people we are meant to be. Someone who has deeply developed their own charism can support and guide us by their example. Who are some of your spiritual role models? Knowing this, a decision or new path may become clearer as we ask ourselves, "What would Jesus or Buddha or my grandfather or my 6th grade teacher do?"

Consciously emulating someone, or a number of someones we admire, often results in acting and thinking more like that person. At times we may even reflect them unconsciously! I recently had an experience with a church body that is moving in such a direction.

Aidan of Lindisfarne, in Northumbria, was a Celtic saint of the 7th century. I see his charism as "inclusiveness," which means "including all, including the extreme limits." Aidan's living out his charism resulted in empowerment of the marginalized. As a monk at the monastery of Iona, he listened to the report on Northumbrian people given by Corman, the monk who had been sent to convert them to Christianity. Bishop Corman returned in frustration, calling the Northumbrians intractable and stubborn. Any mission to them was doomed, even though their king was Christian and had lived on Iona for a time.

The monks listened and then Aidan spoke out. He suggested that talking to people about spirituality needed to be undertaken slowly and gently, showing respect for people as they were. To Aidan's surprise, the other monks immediately voted him a bishop and gave him the mission to Northumbria.

Although his base was at the monastery on Lindisfarne Island, he believed in going to the people rather than having the people come to him. Accordingly, he was usually away from home. He walked most places so that he could more easily interact with his flock. Instead of using the money and goods he was given to make his position as bishop more impressive, he gave most of it away to the poor.

Aidan is known for buying slaves, setting them free and offering them education. He taught the laity spiritual practices that had been reserved for religious, such as reading scripture. Justice was extremely important to him and when he was aware of a wrongdoing, with no concern that he was disturbing his source of donations, Aidan would reprimand the wealthy, including the king, in public.

About five years ago, St. Aidan's United Church in Victoria, British Columbia, decided to examine the roots of the saint they were named for. Rather than focusing on Aidan, some members of the congregation began to explore Celtic Christianity. A day-long workshop was led by Anglican author and scholar Reverend Herbert O'Driscoll. New banners and altar cloths were created using Celtic symbols. A few new hymns were introduced. That's all that was done consciously.

Yet over the last few years, St. Aidan's congregation has been increasingly visible in the greater community as a church who accepts those who may not be acceptable to other faith communities because of mental or emotional challenges, lifestyle, or sexual orientation. St. Aidan's offers many programs for healing and growth, including but not limited to teaching various unfamiliar spiritual practices; offering alternate types of worship, such as a mid-week after work contemplative Holy Communion service; and providing a monthly healing service with laying on of hands.

Members of the congregation are very visible in marches and other protests about injustice. Recently, a conference "Promoting the Culture of Peace," with international speakers, was in danger of being cancelled because registration would not meet expenses at the original location. A member of St. Aidan's congregation heard of this and swung into action. Information was sent out about the change in venue and more than 500 people attended the church over the five-day event.

Other faith communities undertake many of these ministries. Yet I was struck by the close parallel to the ministry and focus of Aidan of Lindisfarne. I spoke recently with one of the ministers about this connection and asked if it was conscious. He responded, "No it isn't. I don't know very much about Aidan. But now I'm going to do some research." A few weeks later, he called and asked me to share a sermon with him, speaking of the similarities we had discovered.

I believe the discernment process we find most effective carries the flavor of our charism. When I asked Franciscan priest Paul Surette about discernment, his example demonstrates how his choice echoes Francis of Assisi's charism. Francis is known for being an "ecologist," recognizing all of creation as family. He cherished this interconnectedness through encouraging the qualities of simplicity, peace, and poverty or littleness, which expresses itself by walking lightly and humbly on the earth.

FATHER PAUL SURETTE'S STORY

I directed a retreat center for ten years: organizing programs, facilitating retreats, giving spiritual direction. At the center I came into close contact with the Alcoholics Anonymous movement. AA impressed me. I saw healing and growth in person after person who followed their 12-step program.

The AA program works. It is a no-nonsense, honest spirituality that is basic and solid. In fact, being faithful to these 12 steps can be a matter of life or death for anyone suffering from a serious addiction. I soon became aware that these 12 steps can work for all of us. The prerequisite is to admit our own powerlessness over that which is controlling us, whether it is a substance or our selfishness, our ego.

So I began to practice the 12 steps myself. Then I started encouraging the people who came to me for spiritual direction to try it. They often said, "I don't have a problem with alcohol!" I explained to them that we would find what was controlling them and restricting their response to God and use that.

The 12 steps are very Franciscan. When I want to discern something, I use these steps. I pray to the Most High for guidance and then look to see if a certain path is interesting to me for self-centered reasons that do not embrace peace, simplicity, or poverty.

The 12 Steps

1. We admit we are powerless over _____, that our lives are unmanageable.
2. We believe that a Power greater than ourselves can restore us to sanity.

3. We have made a decision to turn our will and our lives over to the care of God as we understand [God].

4. We are making a searching and fearless moral inventory of ourselves.

5. We have admitted to God, to ourselves, and to another human being the exact nature of our wrongs.

6. We are entirely ready to have God remove all these defects of character.

7. We humbly ask God to remove our shortcomings.

8. We have made a list of all persons we have harmed, and are willing to make amends to them all.

9. We will make direct amends to such people whenever possible, except when to do so would injure them or others.

10. We continue to take personal inventory and when we are wrong promptly admit it.

11. We are seeking through prayer and meditation to improve our conscious contact with God as we understand [God], praying only for knowledge of [God's] will for us and the power to carry that out.

12. Having had a spiritual awakening as a result of these steps, we try to carry this message to others, and to practice these principles in all our affairs.[76]

The examples I have given of charism are Christian. Many other faiths speak of the benefit of finding someone who inspires you to seek and open to God more fully. The Buddha suggested, "converse with them, serve them, observe their ways, and imbibe by osmosis their spirit of love and compassion."[77]

Huston Smith speaks of the plethora of Hindu gods and goddesses as "matchmakers whose vocation is to introduce the human heart to what they represent but themselves are not." (Smith, p. 35) Each image of Brahma – the Godhead – is a symbol of one aspect of the divine, as it is impossible to think any one can contain the Whole. A Hindu often is attracted to the charism of one of these images of God and forms "a life long attachment." "Only so can [the image's] meaning deepen and its full power become accessible. The representation selected will be one's *ishta*, or adopted form of the divine." (Smith, p. 36)

God speaking through creation

I asked the earth, the sea, and the deeps, heaven, the sun,
the moon and the stars...
My questioning of them was my contemplation,
and their answer was their beauty
They do not change their voice, that is their beauty,
if one person is there to see and another to see and to question...
Beauty appears to all in the same way,
but is silent to one and speaks to the other
They understand it who compare the voice received on the outside
with the truth that lies within.
ST. AUGUSTINE[78]

Some people experience the divine presence most potently in the world around them. Aboriginal, Celtic, Wiccan, and Franciscan spiritualities are particularly known for cherishing creation as sacred. Celtic spirituality suggests we become aware of how we receive divine guidance from the "Big Book of Creation," as well as from the little book of holy scripture.

J. Philip Newell, in *The Book of Creation: An Introduction to Celtic Spirituality*, speaks of the gift of our creatureliness.

This is not to say that what is shown in a creature is the essence of God, for God is essentially unknowable. Rather, what is manifested is an expression of God's essence. Nothing in creation exists in and by itself. The soul of every creature is derived from the one Soul. God, therefore, is not simply in every creature but is the essence of every creature. At heart, creation – including our creatureliness – is a showing forth of the mystery of God.[79]

HENRI'S STORY

I caught up to Henri in late summer as he was coming in from the garden, one of his passions. This was a transition space for him. Soon he would be gearing up for another passion: being present for the spiritual needs and issues of young people as part of an interfaith university chaplaincy.

I am often invited to the path where I can more fully live divine will through nature. An example is the process by which I knew God wanted me to accept the university chaplaincy position. Traveling to the job interview by airplane and ferry took most of a day. I am generally sensitive to and delight in God's presence in nature. This day, however, the divine was "singing" to me through the land and ocean, the sun and sky. The sunset sparkled with vividness. Nature's colors were brighter and richer. God was reaching out to me with increasing beauty as I drew nearer to my destination. As my mind turned to the upcoming interview, I felt a dynamic rightness and a click deep inside me that affirmed this decision.

My discernment process involves starting on a path or decision that seems right, and then being as receptive as possible, trusting that I will be shown whether this is truly the way. I know the correct path for me at that time because it is the one with the most beauty. Connecting with the divine so strongly through nature, I feel my vision is then closer to God's way of seeing. At that time, I usually experience the affirming "click."

VANESSA HAMMOND'S STORY

"Ah, Mary, what should I be doing with these broken eggs: a sensible scramble or a lovely, light cake?" I was nine, living in Ireland, and it was the first time I was consciously aware of a discernment process. It seemed so natural to me that our neighbor would speak to Mary, mother of Jesus, as a friend, wondering about God's will for the eggs accidentally dropped on the kitchen floor.

I often visited that kitchen. There was always a warm welcome for the little Protestant child from "the house" in that

Catholic household. I remember they were poorer than we were, but with a wealth of children and of love. There was lots of love in our house too. And God was always overtly present.

At home, every Sunday lunch involved even the youngest children discussing the sermon from that morning. My father's close friend, a Muslim scholar, often came to visit (once with his five wives) and there were long discussions of spirituality. My father spoke fluent Arabic and would read to me from the Qur'an. My education included Hindu, Muslim, Catholic, and Church of Ireland day schools when I was young, and a Methodist boarding school in later years. I remember how deeply spiritual my Methodist science teachers were. They emphasized the sacredness of all creation, including the process of evolution.

I lived Celtic spirituality for many years before I was aware of the term. As a little girl, my father would take me outside and explain how God speaks to us through many different ways, such as the wind. When I want to discern the path to take, I need to get grounded. That usually means going outside, and even in cold weather taking my shoes off. I need to touch God's creation.

In my early 20s, I was faced with a large and difficult decision. Should my husband and I and our young children stay in Ireland or emigrate to Canada. It looked like the signs were pointing to Canada, but I was having second thoughts. I loved Ireland so much.

I needed to immerse myself in the tactileness of God's creation and to allow the correct path to surface. Borrowing the horse next door, I rode along the beach with my two young ones sitting in front of me. I held up all my conflicting feelings as we trotted into the surf, salt spray wetting our skin and clothes.

As I became grounded, it felt like my thoughts and ideas became cleaner. I moved from jumbled thoughts to one, and the "knowing" was there: "Go ahead, it will be okay." We came to Canada. And it *was* okay.

SISTER DOROTHY BOB'S STORY – MEDICINE WHEEL

I was born to the Fountain Band in Lillooet, British Columbia, and have been a Roman Catholic sister for 42 years. The discernment process the Creator has called me to reflects both faith traditions. It opens me to a path that promotes wholeness, harmony, and balance. When a problem or choice is facing me, I first pray to God, asking for guidance around this issue. Then I draw a medicine wheel. The medicine wheel is a circle of wholeness with four segments representing the physical, mental, emotional, and spiritual, and the four laws the Creator gave us to live by: respect, strength, sharing, and gentleness.

Within these four laws are the seven gifts of the Holy Spirit. They include respect, bravery, love, wisdom, honesty, humility, and truth. After I have drawn my medicine wheel, I open myself to each of the gifts as I think of the object of my discernment. I take each of the gifts of the Spirit in turn to determine which option is more in alignment with it. Does one choice show more respect than the other? What about wisdom? Is it just head wisdom or is the heart involved as well?

I take time to let the Spirit lead me to clarification around each one. At times it is very clear which option will bring me more deeply into right relationship with our Creator. Sometimes much patience is needed before I see the path. Maybe there is a third option that will present itself later, if I am patiently receptive.

Many scientists have been quoted as saying that the more they have studied nature, the greater became their belief that all creation was the result of a loving Creator. We live in a beautiful world. Sufi Kabir Helminski defines beauty as "anything that becomes our point of contact with Love."[80]

Discernment tools

The Christian disciples were trying to decide whether Joseph or Matthias
was to fill the opening in their ranks created by Judas Iscariot's betrayal.

Then they prayed and said, "Lord, you know everyone's heart.
Show us which one of these two you have chosen
to take the place in this ministry and apostleship
from which Judas turned aside to go to his own place."
And they cast lots for them, and the lot fell on Matthias.
ACTS 1:24–26

This is a difficult section for some people due to beliefs that "our ways are right, but the stranger's ways are wrong." Every dualism carries with it a flavor of violence. One side is not viewed with the importance or worthiness of the other. I saw a large moving van the other day with a slogan painted on its side: "We have separate containers, so your prized possessions are not in contact with someone else's junk."

Some people view discernment tools in a negative light. I believe that God is in everything and may choose to speak to us out of anything. Many people *do* feel called to tools of divination, such as the I Ching, runes, Tarot cards, pendulums, etc. If you feel attracted to such a method, it may be useful to keep some points in mind.

- Some people use these tools because they feel a sense of power or control in the decision-making process. This ego need will make it difficult to hear the small, still voice of Spirit.
- Since the tools are concrete, giving a visual message, it can be more tempting to take it literally. We have already discussed the dangers of this.
- A divination tool gives the sense that God's will for us can be elicited any time we use the method. Even though God is always speaking to us, Holy Mystery may not choose to speak to us in this manner, at this

time. And yet, due to the nature of the tool, we have received a visible reading. What does this mean? The following suggestions may help.

○ Discernment may be fun at times, yet it is not a game. Often this type of tool is used by a group in a party atmosphere. If you are serious about hearing God speak to you, approach the process with reverence.

○ Develop a familiarity with the technique. Learn to use the tool appropriately. Understand how others have used it.

○ Begin with a spiritual practice to open yourself more fully to God's voice.

○ Clarify your question or issue.

○ Be receptive and flexible about how the divine may touch you during the process.

○ After receiving a message, take time to let it work in you. Use other procedures such as journaling or talking with a spiritual friend to help clarify what you have heard.

○ Watch to see how your message is affirmed in other ways over subsequent days.

ORACLE AT DELPHI

Apollo, the god of light and reason, was worshiped at Delphi. People coming to consult the Oracle, the word of Apollo spoken through priestesses, took a number of steps to purify and open themselves to receive guidance. First, they made the pilgrimage to Delphi, which for most was long and arduous. Upon reaching the temple, a ritual sacrifice was made of a sheep, goat, or honeycake. Then the seeker ritually washed in a special spring. Now the waiting began.

Patience was needed; the Oracle could not be approached until the seeker was summoned. Above the gateway leading into the temple were etched the phrases "Know Thyself," and "Everything in Moderation." After the time and energy spent getting to the temple and preparing oneself to hear the message, most people would have clarified some aspects of it already. They would be very motivated to hear the guidance of Apollo, and hopefully, receptive enough to let go of their own agenda.

Finally entering the room of the Oracle, the seeker wrote questions on lead tablets, which were given to a priestess sitting behind a curtain. The priestess had made her own preparations of purification and alignment, and now entered a trance where she spoke often unintelligible answers. Translators, in the form of temple priests, wrote poetry based on the priestesses' utterances. "The poetic interpretation was inevitably obscure and ambiguous, but still considered to be the ultimate authority,"[81] says Phil Cousineau, author of *The Art of Pilgrimage*.

Author and scholar Alexander Eliot says, "The real secret lies in the riddling nature of the Oracle's response. They left a wide margin for error, but that is not the main point. They opened up the same margin for the sense of wonder to fill in."[82] The Oracle's words pointed the seeker to the "underlying mysteries of existence. So the eternal paradox of faith – certainty resting on mystery – seemed resolved at Delphi in some very direct way."

LESLIE BLACK'S STORY

I am a certified Healing Touch practitioner. I use my hands as a form of prayer, allowing God's healing power to flow through me to address imbalance and to restore harmony in the body/mind/spirit of my clients. In my training through Healing Touch International, I was taught to use a simple tool called a pendulum as one of the ways of assessing the needs of clients.

Any small object hanging from a string or chain can be used as a pendulum. When I hold it still over various parts of a client's body, I am shown by its movements the places I am called to focus my hands in the treatment session. I believe the Holy Spirit is showing me, via the pendulum, dynamics in the client's energy field that are ready for healing.

When I begin working with a person, I first attune more fully to God and ask that divine will be done for this client and that I be guided to facilitate whatever healing God has for this individual this day. This is the same process used in many faith traditions where healing ministries are being reclaimed as taught by their founders.

My particular faith tradition is Christian. I am also a practitioner and instructor of Naramata Centre's Healing Pathway, which is a Christian adaptation of the Healing Touch International program. "Laying on of hands" is an ancient Christian practice that is being reclaimed today. My work with clients is only possible because of the guidance I constantly receive as I offer myself as a vessel for God's healing power.

I find that frequent prayer and meditation time, where I ask that all areas of my life be aligned with God, helps me surrender my own ego. The more I am able to get my ego out of the way, the clearer the guidance I receive! A pendulum only works as a tool when I am able to get both my ego and my mind out of the way – that is, when I am sincerely open to the message being divinely given.

I also use the pendulum, amongst other methods, to discern my own path in the everyday decisions of life. I often wear a pewter angel around my neck to remind me that my intention is to be aligned with God in all areas of my life. And then it is available as a pendulum for decision-making. I ask the pendulum to move back and forth for "no" answer from God and a clockwise circle for a "yes." I may then use the pendulum to clarify the answer I get, or I may move into another way of discerning.

One day recently, I was feeling overwhelmed by all the pulls on me: as mother of two young children, spouse, educator, and healing practitioner. In prayer, I got a strong urge to go on a retreat, but despaired because it wasn't possible to take time away from all my responsibilities. With use of the pendulum, I clearly got the message that I could clear my schedule that very day for several hours and take some prayer time at the local retreat center. Those few hours were just what I needed and I came home energized and feeling balanced. Another confirmation that God wants what is best for me! If I listen, God can show me a path that I might not see.

Using the pendulum is not a discernment method for everyone. It does require getting our own agenda out of the way or we can run the danger of influencing it with our ego and mind. God speaks to me in very many ways and sometimes I feel called to using a pendulum. You may find you need to practice using it if you feel called to this particular tool.

BOB'S STORY

Because of a number of experiences during my childhood, I became an adult who did not feel safe in the world. Spirituality was important to me, although I stayed away from any organized religion, remembering the judgmental God I had been taught to fear and the judgmental people who spoke demeaningly about other faiths. I was drawn to the spiritual practice of meditation; so I became initiated in Maharishi Mahesh Yogi's Transcendental Meditation during the early 1970s.

In an attempt to feel a personal security, I also explored martial arts. My value system did not accept fighting for offense; I was fascinated by the beauty and power of these ancient methods of self-defense. For many years I read books about martial arts, watched adventure movies, and took courses in a number of techniques.

Surprisingly, my sense of personal safety was not greatly enhanced. One day in meditation I received an inner knowing. "You can train all you want in an attempt to become safer in the world, without achieving your goal. Instead, put your intention and energy into being connected with the divine." The sensation I experienced with this knowing was profound.

I stopped seeking for security in external techniques. My meditation changed too. Now I begin my meditation time with the following words: "I open to the healing Light of God's creative Love." Then I sit with receptivity and gratitude, following the inner felt sensations. I trust that God will give me the experiences I need to heal and grow me.

God gives me guidance through a wide range of inner and outer knowings. One way I feel called to a few times a year is the I Ching, the Chinese Book of Changes. Recently, my teenage daughter has been "trying her wings" and asking for more space to fly. Although I know this is normal, I have been trying to decide how much flying room to give her. I want to find a balance between her level of comfort and mine.

God and I have been working on this issue for a while. A few nights ago I decided to consult the I Ching to hear what God would tell me through that medium. I used *The I Ching Workbook*, by R. L. Wing. I threw the three coins six times, which resulted in the reading "Calculated Waiting" for the present time, leading to "Potential Energy" for the future.

In the reading for the present time, the following statements resonated with me.

Shifting powers are generating new ideas, animosities are appearing, alliances are forming, systems are breaking down, and collective causes are being organized. It is the eternal flux of change as manifested in human affairs...the elements involved are not directly under your control...If you worry about it you will grow inwardly confused and succumb to chaos and fear. You will waste valuable energy through agitation...Inwardly bide your time and nourish and strengthen yourself for the future. Through careful observation attempt to see things without illusions or fears...Keep your thoughts and words on a positive note and maintain an assured and cheerful attitude.[83]

If I follow this guidance and relate to my daughter with patience and cheerfulness, this stance will encourage "Potential Energy." The statements that spoke to me in this reading included the following.

You possess a storehouse of potential psychological energy. There is no reason that it should not be used in a positive exchange. Personal relationships could blossom overnight...Pay particular attention to the continuing development of your character. The totality of what you have experienced has organized itself into an illuminated perspective of great clarity. This may be a real breakthrough in the maturing process. You have the Potential Energy for an enlightened insight that could change your life. (Wing, p. 84)

I felt very reassured after reading the hexagrams. They echoed my life patterns at this time. The suggestions for moderation and acceptance of what is fit in with other guidance I had been receiving in prayer and through people I respected.

This section gave three examples of discernment tools. Prior to using one of the great variety of these tools it is useful to ask the question, "Am I being called to this method of discernment?" Some years ago, after hearing a friend describe how much guidance she received by "sticking her finger in the Bible," I decided to try what seemed an easy way to discern. I received Nehemiah 8:10: "Go your way, eat the fat and drink the sweet wine and send portions of them to those for whom nothing is prepared, for this day is holy to our Lord." Now this reading pleased part of me mightily. I had been eating as healthily as possible because the doctor told me my weight was putting my health at risk. Was this permission to buy a chocolate cake? It didn't take too much reflection to see that I was not to take this reading at face value and, furthermore, that I hadn't been called to this method of discernment.

God with skin on

*Too often we look for sensational signs of God's love
when all we have to do is look to the person next to us.
To some degree God means for us to answer each other's prayers
so as to bring each other into the realm of the sacred
and there find the only true, lasting fulfillment.*
CARMEN L. CALTAGIRONE[84]

Sometimes the divine answers our spoken or unspoken questions through other people. Strangers, friends, family members, even enemies may be used. The information can come without the other even knowing they are an agent for the holy. Or a message for us may come through someone we seek out whom we believe has the ability to intentionally connect with the sacred. Also, someone may seek us out because they receive a message for us from God.

Remember that when God speaks through others, they filter the message through their personalities, needs, emotions, etc. Children play "Gossip," a game where one person whispers a sentence to the person beside them, who whispers it to the next, until it has been passed through everyone in the group. The last child says the message out loud and usually everyone bursts into laughter. Rarely has the message stayed the same. What started as "The chickens are laying lots of eggs this summer" may end as "My children's legs are long this summer." Not so funny, though, if a message from God is scrambled.

REBECCA'S STORY

At 18, I was thrilled to be a nursing student at a large hospital. I had been somewhat sad to leave my family and small community where I was known and loved, but the excitement and opportunities of my new life were very appealing. One advantage was being able to attend Mass more often – daily if I wished.

One day, leaving the chapel, I was stopped by a nursing sister. This older woman said to me, "Rebecca, I have been watching you at worship. You have a religious vocation. You should stop your nursing studies and move to our novitiate. If you don't answer the call now your vocation could be lost!"

I was stunned. Why would God tell this woman what my life path was, without also telling me? How could this woman be so sure? Maybe God was talking to me through this sister because I was not listening properly. I told the sister I would pray about it and escaped.

Once I was alone, I realized that the thought of a religious vocation had been gently nudging at my heart. However, I did not feel drawn to that nursing sister and her religious community. I was confused by the sister's forcefulness in telling me to leave the hospital in case I "lost" my vocation. If God was truly calling me to this life, would there only be the one chance?

I asked God repeatedly for direction. There was no sign I could see. The nursing sister talked about religious vocation every chance she got. If this was the sign God was sending, why did I feel so hesitant?

One day, Sister suggested that we make a novena to the Holy Spirit together. A novena is a prayer for a specific purpose repeated each day for nine days. Often a saint or angel is asked to help with the request for healing or discernment. This suggestion appealed to me. Giving myself to the structure of the novena, I was able to let the question go during the rest of the day. So I stopped worrying at it.

About day five, I realized I was feeling an increased sense of peace with the thought of a religious vocation. I also felt that God was saying to me, "Stay here and finish your nursing training; there will be plenty of time later to become a sister." There was a sense of confirmation that this sister's community was not the one for me. Filled with this peace, I was able to firmly tell the sister what I had discerned.

Then I let the future go and lived as fully as I could in the present. Nearly a year later, I met a woman who had recently spent some time with sisters of another community, on retreat. As I listened to this woman's experience, my heart felt full, and I knew that this was the path for me. It felt even more "right" when I realized that the community's patroness is a saint with whom I had always felt very connected. Over 40 years have passed and I am still happy and grateful to be called to this path.

Others may tell us they speak God's will for us. We need to keep in mind that they are listening the best they can and that ego, dysfunctional patterns, ignorance of the dynamics of a situation, and cultural or familial mindset may disrupt the clarity of their hearing or knowing. If it doesn't feel or seem right for you, wait. God will find other methods to inform you.

At times, we receive messages or answers from the sacred which we misunderstand or do not believe. No problem. God will keep working with us until we "get the message." All we basically need is our "Yes."

ELIZABETH'S STORY

My husband heard a call to ministry and we moved to a different state where he entered theological college. My own path was not so clear. I had an urge to help people and felt I had the skills to support this desire. I had been studying to be a psychologist, yet my contact with severely emotionally wounded people did not attract me to this type of work.

I could see no other path that would allow me to use my gifts; religious ministry was out because I agreed with my Protestant denomination that women should not be ordained. I felt stuck. While waiting for God to direct me, I supported the family by working as a secretary. My husband's full-time student status allowed me to take free courses at the seminary. I chose a course in hospital chaplaincy since that was the only one with a "hands on" component. The students spent time each week in a large hospital, chatting with patients and following the chaplain around. This was an introductory course, the students did no counseling, but it gave us a sense of a chaplain's role.

One day, I found myself entering a patient's room just behind an female oncologist. The doctor and patient were strangers to me, but obviously not to each other. The specialist said without preamble, "The results are back. You have cancer. Don't cry; I will come and see you later." She then turned and left the room. The patient, who was standing beside her bed, began to sob.

As our eyes met, I instinctively opened my arms and the woman came into my embrace. We sobbed together for five minutes. Then the patient pulled away and looked at me quizzically. I answered her unspoken question: "My name is Elizabeth and I'm a student chaplain here." The patient moved back into my arms and continued crying. After a few more minutes, the flow of tears stopped and the woman pulled away again.

Looking straight into my eyes, she said, "I'm so glad a minister came to see me. And I'm so glad you are a woman." I went into shock. Deep in my soul, I knew that God was speaking to me. I had tried to find God's will within limits I had made, rather than follow the subtle promptings I felt inside. God was asking me to break out of the structure that said women should not be ministers. I would have doubted an inner voice as being imagination. But I couldn't negate the truth I heard coming from this dying woman.

I said my "yes" to God and was then able to hear the Holy speak within me. Spirit said, "You already are a minister," and I realized this to be so. However, there was still knowledge to be gained and accreditation the world would accept to be earned. I needed to change denominations and find a seminary which would take me.

I trusted that this path was do-able but was surprised at how smooth it became. My course ended the next week and I decided to continue as a volunteer to gain more experience and have prerequisites for seminary. The hospital chaplain asked if I would like to be put on the payroll since there were funds available!

Then I applied to seminary and was told that all places were full for the next year. Two weeks later, the college phoned and said a spot had come empty and if I could start that year, it was mine. Furthermore, it came with a scholarship!

After finishing my training and being ordained as a Presbyterian minister, I felt called to return to the small community where my mother lived. I needed full-time work and there actually was a hospital chaplaincy position open, but it was only part-time.

I was listening and trusting more easily now and flew in for an interview. After 20 minutes, the panel asked to be excused for a brief consultation. On their return, they told me that after hearing what I could bring to the position, they decided it would be better to make the job full-time. They asked if I would be willing to take it. Twenty years later, I am in the same hospital and still love being a chaplain.

We expect communication from our Source to be delivered by those we view as highly evolved. Yet divine messages are often sent to us by "unintentional prophets" or by those we judge as unspiritual. Part of the message is, therefore, an invitation to let go of restrictive evaluations and expectations.

Spiritual direction/companioning, soul-friending

To "listen" another's soul
into a condition of disclosure and discovery
may be almost the greatest service
that any human being ever performs for another.
DOUGLAS V. STEERE[85]

Some people feel called to assist others on their spiritual paths. A person with whom you have an intimate spiritual friendship is called an Anam Cara, or soul friend, in Celtic spirituality. The Anam Cara is about mutual supporting, challenging, and loving. Brigit of Kildare, fifth-century abbottess of an extremely large monastery of men and women, said that soul friends are a necessity for spiritual development. The Quaker concept of spiritual friendship also speaks of this type of mutual, informal helping relationship.

There are also formal spiritual relationships. Shamans, pastors, rabbis, seers, or others given a mandate to minister in their faith tradition may be approached to help an individual hear the divine more clearly. Usually spiritual guidance is just one of the roles of this person and such a minister may be contacted for guidance around a specific issue. Often the contact is one time or very brief. A law may be interpreted; a ritual may be performed. The spiritual seeker may be a member of the minister's congregation or may hear about and feel called to consult them.

Gurus, starets, and spiritual directors tend to develop longer relationships with seekers. Gurus are teachers who contract with one or more students to provide teaching and guidance about a specific spiritual path. The student-guru relationship may last years and contact can range from learning a spiritual practice from the guru or a representative and then having no more direct contact, to giving up all material possessions and living with the guru or in an ashram associated with the teacher.

The Christian Orthodox starets also develops a contractual relationship with one or more students. The starets takes on responsibility for the spiritual growth of the student, committing to much intercessory prayer and teaching and other guidance. The student may live with or near the starets and the relationship often lasts years.

The spiritual director may be a religious (clergy, nun, monk) or secular. Spiritual directors often have no other relationship with the seeker. Katherine Dyckman and L. Patrick Carroll, in *Inviting the Mystic Supporting the Prophet: An Introduction to Spiritual Direction*, say that the term spiritual direction "is woefully inadequate, for what we speak of is neither 'spiritual' nor 'direction.'"[86] They suggest that the whole person needs to be the focus of this process and that the real director is the Holy Spirit.

The person who is called to accompany others on their spiritual path in this way prepares for this ministry by being aware of their own relationship with Holy Mystery, undergoing a process of personal growth, and learning a range of spiritual practices. Then, when an individual approaches them to speak of things spiritual, the director can see the other's concerns and desires more clearly and keep their own separate. The director listens deeply with unconditional love to the directee. Thomas Hart, in *The Art of Christian Listening*, says that, "such listening to another can become contemplative prayer."[87]

He also states that, "The purpose of direction will be to sensitize people further to the presence and action of God in their lives, and to assist them to make a fuller and more appropriate response to it." (Hart, p. 32) John English makes a distinction between spiritual direction and psychological therapy, which "aims to bring a person to greater freedom through natural self-knowledge; spiritual guidance aims to bring a person to greater freedom through nurturing the experience of God's compassion."[88]

GERRY AYOTTE'S STORY

As a chaplain in a federal institution, I accompany many prisoners on their often rocky path towards healing and growth. I also companion a few people outside of work, in the tradition of spiritual direction. For a Christian, the key to discernment is the ongoing deepening of an intimacy with Christ – that is with a God who loves us unconditionally, individually and corporately, immanently and eternally, and who invites us to live in and out of love. There have been so many horrifying examples in history, and I see them in my work, of people who felt they were called or sanctioned by God to think and feel in life-denying ways and to commit life-denying acts.

As each of us becomes more familiar with our spiritual practices, our unique gifts, and our unique "call" we discover how the divine is speaking to us. My image for concretizing my own experience of God's "voice" is that of a tuning fork, the instrument piano tuners use to know when the pitch of a note is just right. A tuning fork implies precision and accuracy.

When I sit in prayer, I try to "let go" – to relinquish control – so that the Spirit can draw me to the core of my soul and quietly open me to the knowledge that God is God. When I am receptive to God, I have an awareness of my tuning fork. I believe we all have something like a tuning fork that resonates for each one of us in a unique pitch. This is the intimate voice of God. But it is so easy to lose heart and forget that God's voice is often a soft breeze and not the unequivocal wind.

This experience can be described in many different ways. Some people are not aware they have this kind of "instrument" within them until they are guided to it. As a spiritual director, my hope is that the other person might uncover and listen to their own tuning fork, initially through my own focused authentic and active listening to them.

To me, the most authentic way to discern a call to be an instrument of spiritual direction is communally. The individual who experiences a call to engage in spiritual companioning finds that other people approach him or her. As Tom Hart says, "How then do I know whether I have the gift [of spiritual direction] or not? For one thing, people usually tell me."

During my process of exploring whether God was calling me to companion people on their spiritual path, I remember a dream I had which helped me to see some of the ways my false images of God and of myself were getting in the way of my own growth and ability to assist others.

It was the middle of the night. I was walking through the rain down an empty street, listening to the sound of my footsteps. The light from a street lamp showed me a building which I knew traded in objects which represented sin and brokenness in my life. I was relieved the shop was closed and locked. The lock was one of those combination ones: a keypad with numbers from zero to 10.

"No way I can get in," I thought, with relief. Then, human nature being what it is, I found myself randomly pushing numbers. It felt like I was treating myself and my journey arbitrarily, with disdain and flippancy. The lock clicked and the door opened. "Oh well, might as well look inside." I walked through the darkened shop, congratulating myself that I was looking at the symbols of sin and brokenness, but not engaging with any of them. (Later, journaling and prayerful reflection brought to mind Deuteronomy 30:19. "I have set before you life and death, blessings and curses, choose life so that you and your descendants may live.") During the dream I felt that I was flirting with an infinite availability of death.

Then I noticed a man in a wheelchair who was very busy, moving up and down the aisles, pulling unidentified objects off the shelves and stacking them on his lap. I thought, unlike me, he was actually engaging in transactions with the sin and brokenness, which were coming to feel more and more like symbols of spiritual death. At first I looked down on him with judgment and condemnation. Then my feelings changed to compassion and I realized that he was me.

Later, I realized this dream contained a vital dimension of psychospiritual growth. By affectively moving in the dream from a posture of judgment and condemnation, to one of embracing compassion and love, I was changing my image of both myself and God. I cannot accept that God loves me unconditionally, "without condemnation and judgment," until I first learn to appropriate and embrace my own shadow. I've heard it said that there are only two foundational human experiences, fear and love, and the challenge of becoming fully human and fully alive is to let go of fear and live in love. Karl Rahner tells us that grace is God's self-revelation. The first grace which every spiritual director must be prepared to offer is God as unconditional lover.

ROSALIND'S STORY

Her artwork can be seen in many public buildings and private residences. Rosalind was a full-time artist and when her creativity stopped flowing she felt threatened, depressed, and "at loose ends." Waiting it out didn't help. After a few months, Rosalind was run down physically from not eating well and was psychologically drained. She also felt helpless to change her situation, which greatly frustrated her because she saw herself as a take-charge person, "a warrior" and "a tough nut." She had always consciously cultivated her masculine side and tried to ignore her feminine aspect. She tells the story in her own words.

Finally, I got angry. This allowed me to act and I did two things to move from my stuck place. First, I arranged to charge a large amount of food at the local grocery store and then I committed to completing a drawing a day. Immediately upon taking these steps the realization came that I did not have a clear direction for my life.

Five nights later, at 3 a.m., I was still lying awake. I heard a sudden piercing animal-like scream. Thinking of my pet goat in his stable, I grabbed a pair of boots and ran outside with one of the dogs. I was relieved to find my goat untouched and peaceful.

On the way back to the house, I felt playful and made footprints in the new snow beside the path. Watching a striking display of northern lights, I heard the scream a second time. Looking up, I saw this vision of a full silver moon with a gold eagle in front of it. The gold eagle appeared to me to be very close and screaming. It had been apparently broken. When someone tried to put it together again it had been slightly juxtaposed so that the hard edges of the gold were refracting light on it. And light was coming from inside it and around it and it was a really startling and scary thing. I mean it just looked like it was really damn mad at me.

In retrospect, I was surprised that I looked at the vision for a moment and then calmly went back into the house and fell asleep. Other than flashes of memory the following day, I did not feel or think about the experience until I walked to the lakeshore the following evening. There I found myself meditating, a very uncommon activity for me. The quiet meditational moment released the image and then I became very excited.

I knew my experience was real when I found my footsteps in the snow and knew I had been outside the past night. My niece and nephew arrived for a visit a few minutes later and I told them about my experience, wondering aloud what it could mean. My niece told me of a Métis woman she knew who guided people spiritually.

I decided to connect with the woman. During the few weeks of telephone tag before contact was made, I found myself invited by a friend to a birthday party for the Métis wise woman, to be held in a cabin in the mountains. When I finally made contact with the spiritual guide, I invited her to drive with me to the party, giving me the opportunity to share my experience.

During the drive, the guide drew me out and asked if I had any insights into the symbol myself. I really didn't, though I should have because I'm imaginative enough. But I was just struck dumb by the enormity of it. The Métis woman told me that a ritual was needed to deal with the image. Her instructions did not sit easily with me. I must go into the woods alone and feed the eagle. Prior to feeding the eagle I was to acknowledge that God exists and secondly ask [God's] permission to come into contact with this eagle. All of which sounds simple enough unless you've been a raving agnostic all your life and really egotistical and really inclined to a rational approach to life.

Because I felt stuck and curious about the eagle image I decided to trust and suspend my disbelief and do whatever was suggested. That evening in the mountains, under a full moon, the spiritual guide and I entered the woods with a piece of steak. It was reassuring to have the Métis woman with me. I felt childlike. I felt as though I hadn't anyone to advise me or anywhere to start in order to give me an understanding of God or of whatever mystery this might be.

As we walked to the edge of a clearing, my guide stopped and said, "Well go by yourself because there is a nice open place through the trees there and you won't feel quite so intimidated. And I'll wait here."

I walked alone, deeper into the dark woods, feeling somewhat apprehensive, nervous, excited, and sweaty. In the clearing I halted and made my acknowledgments to God and I made my request to speak to this eagle and then I essentially had a discussion with the eagle. It wasn't prayers so much as some questioning. Then, after placing the eagle's food, I rejoined my guide and wordlessly we walked back to the cabin and to our beds.

The next morning I found the food gone. Returning to the house, I began talking with the women who were present for the birthday party and discovered an extraordinary thing. I had always avoided groups of women and judged the female sex as more superficial than the male. With these women there was a strong sense of comfort, support, and caring. They reminded me of the supportive moon behind the eagle. Quiet and serene. There all the time. Only the eagle was out of whack. And the women were there to say it's okay, "You can handle this."

Driving home after the birthday celebration, my depression and stuckness were totally gone. I thought, with gratitude, of the eagle as a spiritual guide. The Métis woman told me that the eagle is a very masculine figure usually only seen by men. It symbolizes healing and creation.

After the ritual of feeding the eagle, it struck me right away that my own masculine energies were being either misused or had been broken or damaged in some way. Not correctly put back together and were fighting me, or angry, or working against me. And also obliterating some of the quieter, more feminine energies.

For a time, I conducted the ritual often and especially at the full moon. But then I realized that I applied a lot of the power to the idea that both God and the eagle were external to myself. And I'm getting more and more confident that this is an inner process, not an external process. As time went on I felt my masculine and feminine aspect becoming much more integrated and harmonized.

I had my eagle experience over 15 years ago. Today, my discernment method is tied in with meditation. I meditate frequently, usually every time I take a bath. If I want direction, I ask in my meditation for the appropriate people to be sent to guide me. I know and trust that this will happen.

JEAN VANIER'S STORY

Jean Vanier is the founder of l'Arche, an international network of communities for people with intellectual disabilities. Discerning God's will for individuals and for the group is an important part of the l'Arche community. Vanier describes one of his aids to discernment, accompaniment, in his 1998 book *Becoming Human*.

An accompanier is someone who can stand beside us on the road to freedom, someone who loves us and understands our life. An accompanier can be a parent, a teacher, or a friend – anyone who can put a name on our inner pain and feelings. Accompaniers may be professionals or therapists, those who have experience in untying the knots that block us in our development. They may be ordained ministers or other people who have grown in the ways of God, who seek to help us understand each other's humanity and needs, and who help us recognize God's call to communion, inner liberation, and a greater love of self.

Accompaniment is necessary at every stage of our lives, but particularly in moments of crisis when we feel lost, engulfed in grief or in feelings of inadequacy. The accompanier is there to give support, to reassure, to confirm, and to open new doors. The accompanier is not there to judge us or to tell us what to do, but to reveal what is most beautiful and valuable in us, as well as to point towards the meaning of our inner pain. In this way, an accompanier helps us advance to greater freedom by helping us to be reconciled to our past and to accept ourselves as we are, with our gifts and our limits.

I was fortunate to meet Father Thomas Phillipe when I left the navy. He was my accompanier for many years. He was always there when I needed him, especially when I began l'Arche. He never judged me but always accepted me and brought out the best in me. Because I was well accompanied, I was able to open up my heart. I did not keep things hidden within, where they could rot and decay. I was able to name my weaknesses and fears...

The one who accompanies is like a midwife, helping us to come to life, to live more fully. But the accompanier receives life also, and as people open up to each other, a communion of hearts develops between them. They do not clutch on to each other but give life to one another and call each other to greater freedom.

So it was easy for me, in turn, to accompany other people, to trust in them, to remove some of the guilt that weighed on their shoulders, and to help them discover their value.

Accompaniment is at the heart of community life in l'Arche, but it is at the heart of all human growth. We human beings need to walk together, encouraging each other to continue the journey of growth and the struggle for liberation, and to break through the shell of egotism that engulfs us and prevents us from realizing our full humanity.[89]

CATHERINE'S STORY

Although I had to work that summer, I was really looking forward to spending a lot of time with friends. Then my supervisor told me she needed someone to move to our branch in Alaska for a few months. I was her choice. Alaska! So far away. On the other hand, a wonderful opportunity to see a new place and meet new people.

As I thought about it more, however, I realized I didn't want to go at this time. Yet authority had given me this position and who was I to say no. I always wanted to follow God's will in everything I did. Surely my supervisor, to whom I owed obedience, was speaking God's will for me.

I couldn't feel settled though. Since it is important to me to follow divine will without reluctance, I looked for a way to clarify and deal with my feelings. There was a spirituality center close to where I worked. Although I had never been there, I had heard encouraging things about their staff. So I made an appointment for spiritual direction.

Sister Joan started by hearing my story and helping me sort out my feelings and issues. I realized I felt very pressured, thinking I should be obedient. She reminded me that God would be with me whatever road I took. That felt reassuring and I didn't feel as anxious about even examining the issue. My agenda though, was still to let go of my negative feelings and "do the right thing," which was to go to Alaska.

As I explained this to her, Sister Joan asked me not to automatically assume I knew God's will in this. She said there may also be a gift in staying home. If I could stop judging myself and let go of my assumption, we could explore each side more freely. As her words sunk in I experienced such relief! Like a large load had been lifted from me with her words. I left that first session with a sense of peace.

There were four spiritual direction sessions in all. We explored both sides thoroughly through guided visualization. At the beginning of each meeting, we verbalized our intent, praying to be open to God's Spirit in our time together. Then I closed my eyes, and after centering, imagined myself alternately in Alaska and at home. She asked me to be aware of what I felt, saw, and heard. After staying with the visualization for some time, Sister

Joan brought me out and I shared my experience.

When I visualized myself in Alaska, I "felt" fear and isolation, "heard" approval from my supervisor for being obedient, and "saw" a desolate landscape. When I opened to staying home, I "felt" warm welcome, acceptance, mutual sharing, "heard" my supervisor scolding me, and "saw" smiling faces.

In our debriefing, I realized I was making a big assumption about my supervisor. I was viewing her as a judgmental parent scolding a disobedient child. And yet I liked and respected her very much. She always seemed interested in my welfare as a person and employee. Sister Joan suggested I share my feelings, needs, and desires with my supervisor and then make the decision.

When I approached my supervisor and started telling her my concerns, she was astonished. Her perception was that she had offered me this opportunity and since I had listened and had not disagreed to it, she thought I wanted to go. She said she knew others who wanted to go and she was glad I had been able to tell her how I felt. That whole experience taught me how easy it is to automatically equate God's will with authority. From that time on, I tried to become aware of and verbalize my own needs and desires to give those in authority more information. It often helped the decision to be fulfilling to everyone involved.

MARTHA'S STORY

It had been a long road to the point where I walked into the Catholic retreat center to find out about spiritual direction. I was as prepared as I could be. My suit was conservative and everything about me was color coordinated. This was surely the outfit of a serious spiritual seeker. In fact, I soon realized I looked more like a nun than the nun I met!

I also had written outcomes: what I expected in a spiritual director, what I expected from God. A week before I had carefully checked to see if I would be acceptable. To my question "Do you help Protestants?" the voice on the phone replied, "Of course we do; anyone can come here."

One of the first things Sister Mary said to me was startling. "I have a list here of spiritual directors you might want to check out." She then described each of their ways of working; some directors were Protestant some were Catholic. "Well," I replied, "I certainly don't want a Protestant director." Sister Mary drew herself up and firmly stated, "This is not about religion, Martha."

I had been a Protestant all my life; I knew Protestants. We were pretty normal people. Catholic nuns, on the other hand, seemed much more credible, dedicated, and must be better at directing people's spirituality. And I certainly needed direction.

There had been a great deal of adversity in my life. Growing up the oldest of seven in a poor family. Our house burned down when I was ten. With no insurance, we initially relied on a supportive community for housing and financial support. Later, as a young mom, my husband had a massive heart attack and died. Then government cuts in health care meant the loss of my meaningful nursing position. These were only a few of the losses in my life.

I couldn't have lived with all those losses without the knowledge that God was with me. Often I felt like I was being protected. And I frequently wanted help from God. Discerning God's will for me, though, was not something I thought of. My prayers were like grocery lists. After deciding what I wanted to do, I would pray that God would help me carry out the decision.

After I lost my nursing position, I accepted the relocation counseling that was part of my severance package. The relocation counselor heard my story and suggested I see someone for grief counseling due to the many losses I had experienced. I was livid! Who was *she* to decide I had unresolved issues!

Yet shortly after, I made an appointment with a grief counselor. It was a beneficial experience, especially the "care plan" she asked me to complete. I had done many of these for patients and taught nursing students to complete them, but of course would never have thought to do one for myself. The counselor asked me to consider all aspects of my life, including the spiritual. At that time I didn't know the difference between religion and spirituality. I saw spirituality as very action oriented. A person prayed, was active in church, and lived a decent life.

As I thought more deeply about my spiritual dimension, however, the realization came that I wasn't happy. I also found a discrepancy between what some people in my church said they believed and how they acted towards each other. I was in cognitive dissonance. I thought the way out of my dissatisfaction was to find the right church, one where people would be congruent.

I started scanning the church section of the newspaper each Saturday, looking for the title of a sermon that seemed closest to my issue of the day. That's the church I would attend that week. Then, treatment for breast cancer intervened and I was unable to church shop for a while. A close friend who I saw once a year, visited and said, "What are you doing about your spiritual growth?"

When I told her I was still looking outside me for the "right" spiritual home, she suggested I try spiritual direction. After putting it off for some time, I finally hied myself off to the local Catholic retreat center.

So there I was with Sister Mary. Trying to make the right decision. Armed with my questions and clipboard. Partway through the interview, I stated, "I'd like to come to you for spiritual direction." "I don't think so," replied Mary. I was shocked. "You're a sister. Don't you have to take me?" "No I don't," she told me. "But I like what you're saying. You're right up front." There was a pause. She didn't look like she was softening. "What would I have to do for you to take me?" Mary smiled: "You'd need to sit a lot looser in the saddle. You're so goal-oriented, living in your head. I don't think I'm the director for you."

By now I was determined to have her as my director. I was confused about what she was saying, yet sensed that she had something I needed. After more discussion, Sister Mary agreed to a three-month trial. Our agreement nearly fell apart when I informed her that I assumed we would have an outcome for each session and would evaluate our progress at the end of each meeting.

As I left that first session, Mary asked me to think about my image of God and we would talk about it next time. I was never in such a snit in my entire life! My image of God! What would I say? Then I realized I had quite a good library. The project looked more doable. I threw myself into study. I wanted to ace this assignment, get it right and show her what a good directee I was.

My subsequent image of God was very detailed. I came in with it neatly written out and thought she would quiz me. I wondered how she would evaluate my assignment. But it wasn't like that at all. Mary does unconditional love well. She didn't judge me for my rigidity and didn't judge my assignment. I started to see that the questions she asked were to clarify and open me to my spirituality. I hung in, even though I was very uncomfortable with the ambiguity.

Then Mary told me that she would assist me to develop a personal relationship with God. Just a minute here! I didn't know if I wanted to go there. I was used to praying the scripture every morning for an hour, but felt I was bringing God into my awareness on my terms. A uncontained God felt threatening.

As we continued to meet monthly, we explored many questions. How has God been for you? Where has God been for you? Where do you notice God in people, in nature? What were the deep insight times, the "Aha!" moments in your life? I moved from anxiety about developing a relationship with this God, to feeling more comfortable. Then, as my spiritual life deepened, I started thirsting for relationship.

Over the next five years, I was drawn to more experiential workshops and retreats. I also completed the 19th Annotation, St. Ignatius's Spiritual Exercises spread out over a ten-month period. I met with Sister Mary weekly throughout this time. Now my spiritual journey feels more solid. I act much more consistently out of compassion towards myself and others. God is "out of the box." I try to discern all the time and my decisions are God-centered now.

The last four stories describe interactions with people who have been called by God to "tend the holy." These spiritual companions are very different and yet each one demonstrates how the divine works through human beings – "God with skin on" – inviting seekers to a personalized path of healing and growth.

Angels

Every blade of grass has its Angel
that bends over it and whispers, "Grow, grow."
THE TALMUD

Scanning the shelves of the spirituality section of even the smallest bookstore, you will discover a book on angels. Stories by and about these messengers of God are also a popular draw in workshops and on television programs such as *Touched by an Angel*. Some faith traditions place more emphasis than others on intermediaries. Beings such as saints or other ancestors that have been incarnate at one time, and non-carnate beings such as angels, are often asked to help us hear the message God has for us.

PROPHET MUHAMMAD'S STORY

At the time of the prophet Muhammad's birth, the people of the Arabian Peninsula worshiped many gods, spirits, and demons. Rejecting these lesser powers, as a young man, Muhammad went into the desert, a common experience for seekers in all faith traditions, to still himself and to seek a Supreme Being. The archangel Gabriel came to him in the cave Hira and commanded, "Proclaim! (or Read!) In the name of thy God and Cherisher, who created – created man, out of a (mere) clot of congealed blood; Proclaim! And thy Lord is Most Bountiful – He who taught (the use of) the Pen – taught man that which he knew not."[90]

Muhammad obeyed the angel and called people to a spiritual conversion: to belief in one true God and to a life lived in accordance with the virtues of justice, integrity, and mercy. He encountered much hostility and hardship because of his message. He also found people flocking to him to embrace Islam.

Gabriel, as spiritual director, also appeared later to Muhammad in the city of Medina during the holy month of Ramadan.

"Night after night [the archangel came] to recite and meditate on the Qur'an with him. Thus this month becomes a time for renewed self-dedication to God: many people decide to turn back from their mistaken ways, to let themselves be guided aright in the community by the Qur'an."[91]

JUDITH'S STORY

In hindsight, she realizes that she was not responding actively to God's call in her life. For two years, Judith had prayed to be able to adopt another child. She already had a daughter, six-year-old Karen, and, as a single mom, was not likely to give birth to another. And yet two or three children seemed right to her.

So I prayed for a child, thinking one would be abandoned on my doorstep or that I would hear about a child needing to be adopted. It didn't happen. Then I went on a family Advent retreat with Karen. I met a couple with two children from developing countries. This new concept took root and I broadened my horizons.

I still didn't actively do something about this sense of call, though. There were lots of valid reasons for not acting: I was very busy working full-time in a non-profit agency always struggling for funding, raising a daughter on my own, healing from a parasitical infection that lasted a long six months.

As the following Christmas neared, I was still telling God I was ready to adopt a child. In the kitchen about a week before Christmas, I remember the sunlight filtering through the two big windows as I prepared a meal. All of a sudden, I couldn't breathe! Then I had a very strong sense of a presence. I knew it was an angel, don't ask me how, but I knew. It was invisible and so real.

Two hands were on my shoulders and I was physically propelled forward across the kitchen. Then the angel left.

I felt a sense of urgency. Not about the angel, there had been a feeling of peace and safety with this incredible sense of presence. The awareness that had come to me as I was pushed was that I needed to do something right away, that I'd waited too long. I knew it was about adoption.

The week after Christmas, I enrolled Karen in a daily program at the local recreation center. I had no idea how to go about adopting a child and needed time to learn and implement the procedures. So the phone calls began. People I spoke with said that I needed to tell everyone I met that I wanted to adopt, because there was no telling who might be able to give me a lead. So I even told strangers on the bus.

At a meeting, I met a woman who related her brother's story of adopting a child from Haiti. That night I wrote to the mission in Haiti and received a note back thanking me for my interest. The letter said there were no children available at the present time. They'd keep in touch. Some months later another letter arrived with a Haitian stamp. I was in the kitchen as I opened it and found two photographs and a proposal.

My soon-to-be daughter was 18 months old. When she was brought to the mission, Katia was dying of severe malnutrition. Her huge belly and eyes and broken skin were too familiar to us from television and magazine documentaries and ads. But all I saw was her beauty.

Her father had died just before Katia was born and without any type of social assistance, Katia's mother could not feed her. Desperate to save her little one, the mother went from hospital to hospital where she was always turned away. Finally she heard of the mission and brought her dying child to them. Katia fought to live and now she was well enough to be adopted.

I was overjoyed that my prayers were answered. I stood in the kitchen reading and rereading the scanty information they sent me about Katia. At one point, Katia's birth date triggered a memory: December 17, 1988. I recalled, with gratitude, standing in this same kitchen about a week before Christmas 1988 and being pushed by the angel into actively searching for my child!

But that wasn't all. Just before I went to Haiti to get Katia, I talked with a woman who had spent some time there. She told me that the Haitians believe that each person has a number of angels caring for them. There is an angel whose particular task is to seek out help for the person when they are in danger. I had met Katia's angel in my kitchen. My whole search process was so clearly orchestrated by God.

BRAD'S STORY

Brad has already shared with us the story of his spiritual growth, which has led to a reconciliation with God, himself, and others. Part of this story involved an angel.

Just after I realized my wife was dead at my hand, I experienced an intense horror and self-loathing. It was impossible to imagine a future, and although I didn't want to die, I wanted to be dead.

I didn't know what to do. Getting into my car, I drove aimlessly. I wasn't thinking. Then I saw a vehicle larger than mine and turned my car into it. Instead of crushing my car and killing me, somehow my car bounced off the front of the other vehicle.

I got out, feeling dazed. As I was standing by the side of the road wondering what to do, I felt a hand on my shoulder. A voice said, "Brad, just tell the truth and it will be okay." I didn't feel alone anymore. I turned, but couldn't see anyone there. When the paramedics came, I knew what to do however. I could trust the voice and follow the guidance even though my thoughts were still unclear.

The ambulance took me to hospital to check me over. I immediately asked to speak to the police. I told the officers what I had done and they went to my home and found my wife. Some time later, I went to traffic court. The driver of the other vehicle told how I had swerved into him and bounced off his bumper. He then said, "After the accident, I looked over at the other car.

I saw a tall man standing by the side of the road and he had a white light all around him." Hearing this I knew that the person who had supported and guided me was an angel.

My husband, Bob, has many angel books and regularly is drawn to discerning divine will through the assistance of angels. He told me of a few books that have been particularly helpful to him. He says, "When a book includes direct quotes from angels, the messages are so full of love, nourishment, and unconditional support that I find it delightful. No human being could be this pure. *Angelspeake: How to Talk with Your Angels*, by Barbara Mark and Trudy Griswold; and *Angels & Oranges*, by Erin Caldwell, have been particularly useful for me."

People who speak of angel contacts describe the experience as ranging from "awesome," to "so natural it was only later I realized that it couldn't have been a real person." So keep your eyes and ears open for God's messengers.

Group methods

We are the beloved of God, within a beloved community with God.
JOHN ENGLISH[92]

Since we live as part of the vast web of life in this universe, every decision has some effect on the whole. At times this effect is very great, such as when our families, friends, or communities are trying to determine which path reflects most clearly God's will for them.

We have undoubtedly all had experience with someone close to us suddenly confronting us with a decision they have made which has an impact on us. Even if the impact is a positive one, we may feel confused and caught off guard. By encouraging others who are affected by a decision to take part in our discernment process, we benefit from their gifts and from their unique relationship with the divine.

The stories in this section come from a couple whose individual discernment entwines as they walk life's path together, people who used groups to help them listen to Spirit's call, and a church group who used a process to ensure that God's voice was heard throughout their planning and decision-making.

MAARTEN AND NADINA STEWART SCHADDELEE'S STORY

I spoke to Nadina and Maarten in their beautiful waterfront home, Maarnada, a word which is a combination of their names and energies and which means "quiet sea." Nadina is a wellness consultant who hears people's stories and companions them through their process. She says she "is always looking at what creates and sustains a healthy and meaningful lifestyle (body, mind, emotions, and spirit)."

Maarten is an internationally known sculptor in stone and wood, and some of his work lives inside and outside at Maarnada, enhancing the sense of sanctuary that is so strongly felt by those visiting the property. Nadina and Maarten welcome many to Maarnada, for they believe they were given use of this land to provide healing and growth for themselves and others.

Nadina and Maarten are called by the divine to collaborate on many projects. They talked to me about their discernment process. Often, Nadina is led first to a path or project. She tells Maarten what she has discerned. Frequently, some time goes by before Maarten experiences his own leading. It is essential that they both hear Spirit calling them before they act.

Nadina experiences the divine call in many ways. She says,

> One of the most common, is a strong surge of energy that starts from the top of my head and moves quickly down through my whole body. Divine energy can be overwhelming, especially when I feel the energy of the whole vision at once. Thankfully, through past experience, I now trust it doesn't have to be done by tomorrow. I've learned to move gently with it, and then sit with it.
>
> I ask for guidance as to what is the first step to bring the vision into manifestation. For me, it then becomes a one-step-at-

a-time process. That is why the use of the labyrinth and journaling are two methods that have consistently supported me.

Maarten may have guidance dreams or a sudden focusing of his attention that has a sense of rightness about it. Much of his work is commissioned, although if he does not experience inspiration Maarten refuses the project. He told me of a time when he was offered a substantial amount of money to produce a work that seemed quite interesting. Yet the inspiration did not come. Even though Maarten could easily have sculpted what was requested, without the support of divine energy he said no.

Nadina and Maarten told me this last example of discernment during my visit with them. They are very involved in voluntary community service. With so many worthy causes, it is important to discern where to put their time and energy. Nadina says,

During the holidays of Christmas 1999, our friend and neighbor Dr. Charles Ludgate showed me a tiny gold reef knot that was a symbol chosen by the Vancouver Island Prostate Support Group. As I held the tiny lapel pin, it spoke to me in the language of the heart. I felt a connection to the energy of the group of men, their doctors, and their families it represents.

Showing the reef knot pin to Maarten, I asked him if he would create it in Vancouver Island marble. He didn't respond to that or subsequent requests. I trusted that he would receive a message of guidance if this project were to be brought to life. In July, I felt called to ask him again.

Timing is everything. Moments later, we could see Charles, Carol, and their children Alison and David, in their yard watching a backhoe clear a space for a vegetable garden. Maarten went to join the Ludgate family. As he watched, suddenly David turned around and on his green baseball cap was the logo of the Prostate Reef Knot.

Maarten connected the dots or shall I say knots. He felt the knowing inside him that said, "do it," so he mentioned the project to Charles. Charles was delighted and told us about the Capital

Region Prostate Centre opening in the fall. The Ludgates came over to choose the marble and the project was born.

My father, Bill Stewart, died of prostate cancer on October 31, 1985. At the opening of the center 15 years to the day of my father's death, I was asked to unveil "Courage and Compassion," a touchstone of healing. The sculpture honored all those who had died of prostate cancer, their families, those who were going through it now, and the infusion of hope that now comes to those who will receive the possibility of cure and healing. The sculpture was also in gratitude to the medical profession who did the best they could and now are willing to step into community, through this center.

Fifteen years ago I said a prayer and that day my prayer was answered. The stone had created a touchstone to center and focus all of us and the gifts we bring to the healing connection.

RO FIFE'S STORY

I know I have an issue to discern when I experience something in the bottom of my stomach that won't go away. As I focus on it, the issue does not feel integrated into my life. I have a number of spiritual friends in my life who I can go to when this happens. I may feel led to one person or to a group. I know these people will hear me with acceptance and speak as they feel led by the Spirit.

A few years ago, some friends e-mailed me with an opportunity to work on a Guatamalan development project supported by the Canadian Friends Service. It seemed like a golden opportunity to be of service. Yet that "something" was in the bottom of my stomach. I was not clear about its meaning. So I waited, open to hearing how Spirit would give me clarity. Soon after, I felt an urge to take part in a worship sharing group. This group had a specific focus and we each spoke to a statement, which Quakers call a query:

Every stage of our lives offers fresh opportunities. Responding to divine guidance, try to discern the right time to undertake or relin-

quish responsibilities without undue pride or guilt. Attend to what love requires of you, which may not be great busyness.[93]

As I shared, it became clearer that the issue around this new project had to do with boundaries. Because I was living at the Friends' meetinghouse, with my partner and young son, setting personal boundaries was of particular importance. Work was always waiting in the next room. Would this new project encourage me to move past my boundaries? What doors would it close? I left the worship sharing group with my issue more concrete.

Within a month, I attended a women's group which happened to have "boundaries" as the theme that time. As I listened to the other women speak, I heard a diverse range of feelings, issues, and ways of setting boundaries. I began to see that I held a stereotyped view of boundaries which had contributed to the discomfort in my stomach. Taking on a new project would not necessarily move me past my boundaries. I left that group with a greater sense of ease every time I thought of the project.

A month and a half later I still felt at ease. I said "yes." I thoroughly enjoy doing this work. And it has unfolded in ways I could not have foreseen. For example, my partner is now also employed on the project. I am very aware of my boundaries and there has been no problem in this area.

Groups for discernment

Ro used the groups already present in her faith community as aids to discernment. Existing prayer, faith sharing, healing, or other groups may provide a safe structure for you to bring your discernment concern to. A group you are already a member of may be appropriate for this purpose. If you do not belong to a group, with a little research you may be surprised at the variety of groups available in your own faith community or the larger secular community.

If you feel the urge to use a group for discernment, it may be helpful to have a prior check-in with the group facilitator to explain your purpose in attending. That person can then be more intentional in assisting you and can let you know if the group is, in fact, appropriate for such a purpose.

The next two stories describe groups convened specifically to help an individual discern God's will for them.

ROCHELLE GRAHAM'S STORY

I'm someone who sees my work as my call. I love to serve God in community. So when I was trying to decide whether or not to stay in my current job it was a very big question for me. For 25 years I have been a physiotherapist. For the past few years, an increasing amount of my work time was taken up with the Healing Pathway program through Naramata Centre.

I was doing healing work, training, supervising students, and had written a book with Flora Litt and Wayne Irwin called *Healing from the Heart: A Guide to Christian Healing for Individuals and Groups*. This work was consuming so much time that I was reaching a crunch. My physiotherapy hours at the local hospital were not enough to retain my licensing as a physiotherapist. The Healing Pathway program had become so popular that Naramata Centre wanted the position I was in to be essentially full-time.

I loved both types of work, so felt pulled in two directions. Although it might seem like a natural progression to "go with the flow" and do the Healing Pathway full-time, I know that God does not always call us to the obvious path. Since it was essential for me to follow God's will, I knew I needed a discernment process.

In October, I was part of a group reading and discussing a book by Dorothy C. Bass called *Practicing Our Faith*. One chapter was on discernment. An example was given of a Quaker discernment process called a clearness committee. As I read the example, I felt drawn to the process. I heard myself saying, "Oh, this is the way to go about my question!"

Following the process of the clearness committee, I clarified the question I wanted to discern and then prayed about who to have on my committee. I chose people who knew me in the different facets of my life. They included my husband, a person who was involved in Healing Pathway, a physiotherapist, and one person who had gone through a similar group discernment himself. Other than this man, this was a new process to myself and everyone else.

I was surprised and grateful at how smoothly and quickly it went. I thought we would need to meet a number of times. Yet at the end of the first two hour-meeting, the decision was clear. My group listened so caringly and respectfully as I bared my soul. At first it was rather scary. I felt vulnerable, with all the attention on me. Then I relaxed as I felt their interest in helping me to hear what Spirit was calling me to.

Partway through, I started to feel excited and deeply grateful about these people who were giving me their time and attention. Their questions and clarifications helped me to focus more deeply than I could have done alone. It felt like they were holding a mirror up. And the reflection got clearer and clearer, until one of them said, "It looks like you have made your decision."

And I realized I had. I felt a conglomerate of emotion: teary with relief, surprise at my decision and at how the process had facilitated it, and very grateful. God wanted me to go back to physiotherapy.

It was amazing the speed with which my new direction came together. I thought that it would take about a year to find a full-time physiotherapy position. They are just not that common. There was a position at my hospital, with an application deadline of the next day. I had been told about it two days earlier by a number of people who suggested I apply. I kept saying no. I hadn't had my discernment group yet; I didn't know what God wanted me to do.

As I drove home from my clearness committee, I thought about the job offering. I remembered how many people had suggested I apply. It seemed important to pay attention to that. God may be talking to me through others.

The next day I opened my mail and found a letter from the College of Physiotherapists. I was informed that I needed to have 2,000 hours of work as a physiotherapist by the end of the year or I would lose my license. I went to the hospital and put in my application ten minutes before the competition closed.

It would seem to most people that it was very unlikely that I would get the job. It was given on seniority and due to the few hours I had been working, I was very far down the seniority list. With the letter from the College coming the day after the clearness committee, though, all I could feel was gratitude: "Thank you, God, again you're looking after me in ways I couldn't have known." Whether I would get this position or another, I was going in the direction God had pointed out. I knew it would all unfold if I did my part by trusting and staying receptive and flexible. Two weeks later, I heard that the job was mine.

PARKER PALMER'S STORY

During my tenure as dean at Pendle Hill, I was offered the opportunity to become the president of a small educational institution. I had visited the campus; spoken with trustees, administration, faculty, and students; and had been told that if I wanted it, the job was most likely mine.

Vexed as I was about vocation, I was quite certain that this was the job for me. So as is the custom in the Quaker community, I called on half a dozen trusted friends to help me discern my vocation by means of a "clearness committee," a process in which the group refrains from giving you advice but spends three hours asking you honest, open questions to help you discover your own inner truth. (Looking back, of course, it is clear that my real intent in convening this group was not to discern anything, but to brag about being offered a job I had already decided to accept!)

For a while, the questions were easy, at least for a dreamer like me: What is your vision for this institution? What is its mission in the larger society? How would you change the curriculum? How would you handle decision making? What about dealing with conflict?

Halfway into the process, someone asked a question that sounded easier yet [sic] but turned out to be very hard: "What would you like most about being a president?"

The simplicity of that question loosed me from my head and lowered me into my heart. I remember pondering for at least a full minute before I could respond. Then, very softly and tentatively, I started to speak: "Well, I would not like having to give up my writing and my teaching...I would not like the politics of the presidency, never knowing who your real friends are...I would not like having to glad-hand people I do not respect simply because they have money...I would not like..."

Gently but firmly, the person who had posed the question interrupted me: "May I remind you that I asked what you would most *like?*"

I responded impatiently, "Yes, yes, I'm working my way toward an answer." Then I resumed my sullen but honest litany: "I would not like having to give up my summer vacations...I would not like having to wear a suit and tie all the time...I would not like..."

Once again the questioner called me back to the original question. But this time I felt compelled to give the only honest answer I possessed, an answer that came from the very bottom of my barrel, an answer that appalled even me as I spoke it.

"Well," said I, in the smallest voice I possess, "I guess what I'd like most is getting my picture in the paper with the word *president* under it."

I was sitting with seasoned Quakers who knew that though my answer was laughable, my mortal soul was clearly at stake! They did not laugh at all but went into a long and serious silence – a silence in which I could only sweat and inwardly groan.

Finally, my questioner broke the silence with a question that cracked all of us up – and cracked me open: "Parker," he said, "can you think of an easier way to get your picture in the paper?"

By then it was obvious, even to me, that my desire to be president had much more to do with my ego than with the ecology of my life – so obvious that when the clearness committee ended, I called the school and withdrew my name from consideration. Had I taken that job, it would have been very bad for me and a disaster for the school.[94]

COLLEEN AND PAUL'S STORY

Colleen and Paul are members of their church's discernment team for ministry with Children, Youth, and Families. For years, the church had hired two young adult students, on contract, to facilitate youth groups and other activities. Two new students were hired each year, usually from outside the church community. So it took some time for the larger faith community and the students to develop a comfortable working relationship with each other.

For this, as well as a number of other reasons, the setup wasn't meeting the various needs that had been identified by the discernment team. The members realized a new way was needed and yet did not know what path to take. Then they heard about a workshop offered by Chuck Olsen. Four of the team members attended.

Charles M. Olsen is program director and staff mentor at Worshipful-Work, based in the Heartland Presbyterian Center, in Kansas City, Missouri. He has a special interest in discernment in church groups, from small prayer meetings, to committees, to annual meetings of international religious bodies.

The Ministry for Children Youth and Families team decided to use the discernment process outlined in *Discerning God's Will Together: A Spiritual Practice for the Church*, the book Olsen wrote with Danny E. Morris, author of *Yearning to Know God's Will*. The authors describe a ten-phase discernment process that is "like a dance by which a religious group comes to rest on a course of action. In the dance, all of the participants' wisdom and gifts – humility, reason, intuition, tradition, religious practice – are called forth until the Divine Presence breaks in and lights the right path, offering sight and guidance to individuals and the group."[95]

A number of images are used to describe each phase of the discernment process: stepping stones in a reflection pool, movement from seeding to harvesting plants, and a spiral around the magnetic core of God's will. The discernment process begins with "Framing" and ends with "Resting." Framing "identifies the focus for discernment of God's will. The matters to be included are arranged into a unified whole. The focus of the exploration is briefly described." (Morris and Olsen, p. 66)

Resting is a phase which "tests the decision by allowing it to rest near the heart to determine whether it brings primarily feelings of consolation (a sense of peace and movement toward God), or desolation (distress and movement away from God)." (Morris and Olsen, p. 67)

Each phase is clearly explained, with current examples from churches and historic examples from scripture. Questions are suggested to facilitate the phases and common issues and challenges are outlined. The book also includes an historical view of Judeo-Christian discernment, as well as issues that both individuals and groups need to explore to clarify their spiritual path.

Colleen and Paul shared the story of the team's discernment process.

P: Those of us who were meeting about this concern felt like we had come to a dead end. There seemed to be lots of questions, no answers, and little hope. Just having an opening and closing prayer, dedicating the meeting to God, was not enough to give us the sense of where God might lead us in our wandering.

C: It was a very old problem and various people had met about it for years. I came into the meeting knowing others were discouraged, wondering how it could possibly be different. I even felt some guilt, thinking that as chair of the board, it was my fault the team wasn't working.

P: By framing the issue as seeking God's will, we forged a common group identity, healed some hurt relationships, and opened ourselves to a decision to which everyone was committed. We received benefits far above and beyond our expectations.

C: One team member summed it up for the group after we had made our decision. She heartfully stated, "Wow, do I ever feel lighter!" We all felt the team had stayed close to Spirit every step of the way, so we had an easy confidence in acting on our decision. For me, there was the inner sense of peace, which I experience when I know I am following divine will, nothing niggling at me. As we checked around the group, everyone indicated that they felt a deep rightness.

P: The "shedding" process was the most dramatic. "Shedding means naming and laying aside anything that will deter the person or group from focusing on God's will as the ultimate value." The question is asked, "What needs to die in me/us in order for God's gifts and direction to find room in our lives?" (Morris and Olsen, pp. 74–75) The whole discernment took about a dozen meetings over two months and we spent three sessions just on shedding. This part of the process called for deep sharing of our personal investments and preconceptions and we found our trust level growing as a result.

C: In the past, we were nervous about exploring wild ideas, in case the group got off track and we wasted a lot of time or fractured group cohesiveness. Yet we also wanted to hear what God wanted the package to look like and we realized that divine vision could include infinite possibilities. How could we allow ourselves to be guided if we were not receptive to the new, the radical? This process provided a structure that helped us to acknowledge and honor all contributions, while remaining sensitive to the vision.

Same issue – different messages

Sometimes a couple or a group hear what seem to be conflicting messages from God. There is a tendency in some groups to immediately think that one person – the one the group has designated as the sage or the mystic or the minister and so on – must have the "true" word. The others then ignore the guidance they are receiving. This is unfortunate. There can be many reasons for seemingly conflicting divine leadings. This story occurred recently in my own life. Judi, one of my spiritual friends, was involved. Because we are supporting each other on our spiritual paths, at times one friend hears a message for another.

NANCY AND JUDI'S STORY

I received my first pair of eyeglasses at age 18 months. My parents told me I frequently came home proudly holding a new toy or kitten that I had traded for the uncomfortable contraptions. From age three on, I had a number of eye surgeries, the last was when I was in my mid 20s. An ophthalmologist told my mother, in my hearing, that I would probably become blind by late middle age. I was 6 at the time.

My vision stopped deteriorating after the last surgery, much to my relief. I was left with eyeglass lenses as thick as bottle ends, though. Without my glasses, I could not read the numbers on a telephone dial. I traveled frequently, and if I set my glasses down when I went to bed in an unfamiliar place, and forgot exactly where I put them, I could only find them by feel the next morning.

At one checkup, four years ago, my ophthalmologist told me I was an excellent candidate for corneal laser surgery. When my father-in-law heard this, he immediately offered to pay for the procedure. To be free of glasses! I could hardly take in the possibility. Because of my many negative memories of surgery, I felt quite anxious, although not anxious enough to turn my back on the promise of freedom.

Surgery was successful and it seemed that I had entered a new world; I could even read without glasses. Three years later, I realized my vision had slipped. I was needing off-the-counter reading glasses more frequently. Returning for a check up, the ophthalmologist agreed that it would be useful for me to have further laser on my right eye. The repeat surgery was complimentary.

I was given an appointment three months distant and some reading material about the procedure. My friends and family were pleased that I had taken this step. I received a confirmatory peaceful feeling in prayer whenever I opened to the upcoming surgery. One day, though, my friend Judi contacted me and said she had been holding me and my surgery in prayer when she heard, "Tell Nancy not to be a martyr." She asked me if I really needed this surgery.

Her message confused and upset me. I *do* have a martyr tendency, and yet I had been getting feelings of peace about the surgery. I was even more disturbed when I read the material I had been given. This surgery was not expected to produce much change in my vision.

I settled in for a long prayer time and got the familiar peace. Over the next three months, Judi received her message three or four times and I received mine more frequently, because I asked often. I respected Judi's message, especially since the only other times I could remember that she had received a message for me had been when I was missing something.

With such contradictory messages, I didn't see how we could both be hearing clearly. So I attended the pre-op appointment with as much receptivity as possible. How could this conflict be resolved? The technician explained the procedure and the instructions for post-op care. Halfway through I hit pay dirt. She mentioned a condition called "dry eye," which sometimes occurred after surgery. If this happened, tiny plugs would be inserted in my tear ducts to keep fluid from draining.

As she spoke the term dry eye, I experienced a sensation I call "Heaven holding its breath." I feel it at times I am meant to pay more attention to whatever is presently occurring. It feels just like a breath being held, time stopping for a split second. I asked the technician to describe the symptoms of dry eye and everything fell into place.

For over a year, I had put up with eyes that felt like they were full of sand. They itched almost continually. I thought it was stress or eyestrain and tried to rest them more. I went to my doctor who gave me some moisturizing drops. I did not return to her when the drops did not work. I was too busy. So I had given up on searching for relief and endured the discomfort. Real good martyr style.

I asked the technician to test me for dry eye right then. It was no surprise to me that I had a strong case of it. Plugs were inserted in both tear ducts during the laser procedure. After my eyes adjusted to the plugs, there was no discomfort at all. My symptoms were completely gone and my eyesight improved so I did not need the reading glasses. One of the symptoms of dry eye is blurred vision.

If I had interpreted Judi's message from God *literally*, or saw it as right and mine as wrong, I would have canceled the surgery. God would have had to find some other way to bring dry eye to my attention, a more difficult task due to my unreceptivity in this area. If had *ignored* Judi's message, I would not have been as sensitive to the information given to me at the pre-op meeting. The ophthalmologist would have discovered the condition after surgery. I was glad, though, that I had discerned God's communication myself.

No one is given complete information about divine will for themselves or for others. By giving us partial information, God invites us into deeper awareness of our core need to be in relationship.

When discerning is difficult

My God, my God, why have you forsaken me?
Why are you so far from helping me,
from the words of my groaning?
O my God, I cry by day, but you do not answer;
and by night, but find no rest.
PSALM 22

Throughout this book I have tried to place each story in a section where it would illustrate a concept such as "receptivity," or a method such as "prayer." Yet most stories touch on more than one concept and/or method. What they all have in common is God's visible presence, sometimes overwhelming in its intensity, sometimes gentle and subtle. A reader may be left with the impression that the people who lived these stories always hear divine guidance clearly and quickly.

Spending more time with each story brings the awareness that often great patience and perseverance was needed to understand God's will. At times the search was lonely, confusing, or painful. It took Brad, for example, a number of years to build his relationship with God to the point he was able to separate the voice of Spirit from his own ego. Judith repeatedly called to God for a child and it was only after two years that she was able to hear the message that she was off track.

Many of the people in this book speak about mishearing, wandering off the path, and waiting for some time before the guidance is clear. Even with years of experience in discernment, it may be months or years after an event before we are able to see how God was present in it.

Also, everyone's spiritual journey involves wilderness or desert experiences, times when it seems that God has abandoned us. Nothing we can do gives us the sense that God cares, or is even present. People who have walked through this wilderness or desert offer some suggestions to those who will follow in their path.

- Speak regularly with a spiritual guide. If God seems absent in your life, allow support from a human being – "God with skin on."
- Examine your life to see if there are more mundane reasons for feeling disconnected from God. Are you also feeling disconnected from yourself or from others? Being in poor physical or emotional health will affect your spirituality. Any current or past unresolved relationship issue will impact on how we view our relationship with God.
- Flora Slosson Wuellner, in *Heart of Healing Heart of Light*, speaks of "the natural ebb and flow of feeling and awareness. These seasons of the spirit are natural in many aspects of our lives…We each have a unique rhythm of cresting and quiescience."[96] Relationships also have times of ebb and times of flow.
- Read those who have eloquently described their wilderness experience, such as St. John of the Cross. John spoke of his "dark night of the soul" and provides hope by showing how it *does* come to an end.
- Know that God is not giving you this experience as a punishment. Hiding love and support is a human "game" that comes out of low self-esteem. Why do these wilderness experiences occur? We may have an inkling or no idea at all. There may be many contributing factors. Those people who have successfully negotiated the wilderness sometimes say they never knew the reason.
- Continue your spiritual practices even though they may seem dead or unsatisfying. If you become intentionally unreceptive to the divine, it will be more difficult for God to get through to you.
- Look for the opportunity in this time. Katherine Dyckman and L. Patrick Carroll suggest, "Sometimes what appears to be a blockage in prayer is rather a gift of God. Through darkness, aridity, and emptiness we are called to a new form of prayer, a new stage of our relationship with the Lord."[97]

In conclusion

Here I am, Lord. Is it I, Lord?
I have heard you calling in the night.
I will go Lord, if you lead me.
I will hold your people in my heart.
DANIEL SCHUTTE, "HERE I AM LORD"[98]

Discerning during wilderness times means making the best decision you can based on your values and individual preferences. During normal times, use the following suggestions which recurred frequently in the stories.

• Develop a relationship with the divine through spiritual practices. Many people experienced in discernment, suggest that you have at least one spiritual practice which encourages some type of quieting the self to rest receptively in God. These include the many varieties of meditation and contemplative prayer and any practice that moves us towards the scriptural guidance, "Be still and know that I am God."

• Prepare yourself to be an effective channel, through self-awareness and right living.

• Have the intent to be always guided by God, not just around a specific question and concern. Expressing intent in the morning to be led, and spending time at night prior to sleep examining your day, will exercise your discernment "muscles."

• Open yourself to both your graced history and to how Holy Mystery is currently touching you to sensitize yourself to the way of discernment to which you are being called. Many of the stories indicate that God often calls us through our gifts, especially if we are not using or honoring them enough. At times, we may be called through our weaknesses, especially if we have been off balance because we are overusing one aspect of ourselves.

- Cultivate the qualities of receptivity, patience, trust, and willingness to participate with God in love.
- When you experience a leading, seek confirmation through some of the procedures described in this book.
- Think "expansion" rather than "contraction." Look at the sign or message within its context, rather than, for example, taking one sentence or part sentence from scripture.
- Say "thank-you."
- Go out into the world loving and serving our God, who is loving and serving you, in the unique way in which you are called.

You have just had a glimpse into the spiritual lives of 75 women and men. Many of them expressed to me a wish for you, so I feel I am standing with a crowd as I say that I hope the stories and concepts in this book have sensitized you to the presence of our loving God in your life. Sister Pat Bergen, CSJ, has kindly given me permission to end with her discernment blessing for you. I would enjoy hearing any of your discernment stories. I can be contacted via my publisher.

May Wisdom be present in your discernment
shedding light upon dormant dreams and unfolding paths.
May trust invite you to explore the unknown with a hopeful heart.
May supportive companions keep vigil in your waiting.
May you be blessed with patience and courage
in the expression of your true self.
May the yearnings of the Spirit call forth generosity and great love.
And, may your heart be opened always
to welcome holy newness. Amen.
SR. PAT BERGEN[99]

Permissions

Permission to quote:

From *Narrow Road to the Interior* by Matsuo Basho, translated by Sam Hamill, © 1988 by Sam Hamill. Reprinted by arrangement with Shambhala Publications, Inc., Boston, www.shambhala.com

From *Science and Health* by Mary Baker Eddy. Used by permission of publisher.

From *Peace Pilgrim: Her Life and Work in Her Own Words*, © Friends of Peace Pilgrim. Used by permission.

From *Becoming Human*, © 1998 by Jean Vanier. Reprinted by permission of Stoddard Publishing Co. Limited.

From *Confessions of St. Augustine*, translated by John K. Ryan. Used by permission of publisher.

From lyrics to "Healer of Our Every Ill," by Marty Haugen, © 1991 G.I.A. Publications, Inc. Used by permission.

From *Let Your Life Speak*, by Parker Palmer, © 2000 Parker Palmer. Reprinted by permission of Jossey-Bass, Inc., a subsidiary of John Wiley & Sons, Inc.

From "Du bist die Zukunft…/You are the future." by Rainer Maria Rilke, translated by Anita Barrows and Joanna Macy, "Es wird nicht Ruhe in…/There will be no rest in the houses:", from *Rilke's Book of Hours: Love Poems to God* by Rainer Maria Rilke, translated by Anita Barrows and Joanna Macy, copyright © 1996 by Anita Barrows and Joanna Macy. Used by permission of Riverhead Books, a division of Penguin Putnam, Inc.

From "A Question of Balance" by Justin Haywood….

From "Here I Am, Lord" © 1981, Daniel L. Shutte and New Dawn Music, 5536 NE Hassalo, Portland, OR 97213. All rights reserved. Used with permission.

From "On Eagle's Wings," by Michael Joncas © 1979, New Dawn Music, 5536 NE Hassalo, Portland, OR 97213. All rights reserved. Used with permission.

"Holy Wisdom" by Pat Bergen, CSJ, courtesy of Ministry of the Arts, Sisters of St. Joseph, LaGrange, IL. www.ministryofthearts.org

All biblical quotations:

Unless otherwise noted, are from the *New Revised Standard Version of the Bible*, copyright © 1989 by the Division of Christian Education of the National Council of Churches of Christ in the USA. All rights reserved. Used by permission.

Endnotes

Introduction

1. Patricia Loring, *Listening Spirituality*, vol. 1 (Washington: Openings Press, 1997), p. 12.
2. Dalai Lama, *The Good Heart: A Buddhist Perspective on the Teachings of Jesus* (Boston: Wisdom Publications, 1996), p. 79.
3. John J. English, *Spiritual Freedom* (Chicago: Loyola University Press, 1995), p. 264.

Part 1: Concepts

4. Anita Barrows and Joanna Macy, trans., *Rilke's Book of Hours: Love Poems to God* (New York: Riverhead Books, 1996), p. 119.
5. Deepak Chopra, *How to Know God* (New York: Harmony Books, 2000), p. 148.
6. John Shea, *Stories of Faith* (Chicago: Thomas More Press, 1980), p. 65.
7. C. S. Lewis, *Surprised by Joy: The Shape of My Early Life* (New York: Harcourt Brace & World Inc., 1955), p. 224.
8. Martin Buber, *Tales of the Hasidim: The Early Masters* (New York: Schocken Books, 1947), p. 251.
9. Don Richard Riso and Russ Hudson, *The Wisdom of The Enneagram: The Complete Guide to Psychological and Spiritual Growth for the Nine Personality Types* (New York: Bantam Books, 1999), p. 9.
10. Richard Rohr, *Enneagram II: Advancing Spiritual Discernment* (New York: Crossroad, 1995), p. 7.
11. Lois Wilson, *Turning the World Upside Down: A Memoir* (Toronto: Doubleday Canada Ltd., 1989).
12. This is my paraphrase of a story told in *The Teaching of Buddha* (Tokyo: Bukkyo Dendo Kyokai, 1966), p. 40.
13. Abdu'l-Baha, *Baha'i Prayers: Holy writings* (Malaysia: Baha'i Publishing Trust, 1991), p. 21.
14. Flora Slosson Wuellner, *Heart of Healing Heart of Light: Encountering God Who Shares and Heals Our Pain* (Nashville: Upper Room Books, 1992), p. 99.
15. Diarmuid O'Murchu, *Poverty, Celibacy, and Obedience: A Radical Option for Life* (New York: Crossroad Publishing, 1999), p. 88.
16. Patricia Loring, *Listening Spirituality*, vol. 2, (Washington: Openings Press, 1999), p. 69.
17. Nancy Reeves, first published in *Presence: The Journal of Spiritual Directors International* (January 2001).
18. John Shea, *Stories of Faith*, p. 9.
19. Gerald G. May, *The Awakened Heart: Opening Yourself to the Love You Need* (San Francisco: Harper, 1991), p. 173.
20. Isaac Penington, *Works*, vol. 3 (New York: Sherwoods, 1682), p. 520.
21. Danny E. Morris and Charles M. Olsen, *Discerning God's Will Together: A Spiritual Practice for the Church* (Bethesda: Alban Publications, 1997), p. 16.
22. Albert Schweitzer, *Albert Schweitzer: Out of My Life and Thought, An Autobiography*, C. T. Campion, trans. (Austin: Holt, Rinehart and Winston, Inc., 1933), p. 75.

23. Colleen Fulmer, "The 'No' Song," from the album *Her Wings Unfurled* (1989).
24. Peace Pilgrim, *Peace Pilgrim: Her Life and Work in Her Own Words* (Santa Fe: An Ocean Tree Book, 1982), p. 11.
25. Loring, *Listening Spirituality*, vol. 1, p. 154.
26. Helen Bacovcin, trans., *The Way of a Pilgrim* and *The Pilgrim Continues His Way: Spiritual Classics from Russia* (New York: Doubleday, 1978), p. 13.
27. Katherine Dyckman and L. Patrick Carroll, *Inviting the Mystic Supporting the Prophet: An Introduction to Spiritual Direction* (Mahwah, NJ: Paulist Press, 1981), p. 20.
28. Loring, *Listening Spirituality*, vol. 2, p. 25.
29. D. V. Steere, from the introduction to *Quaker Spirituality* (Philadelphia: Religious Society of Friends, 1988), p. 42.
30. Peace Pilgrim, *Her Life and Work*, p. 11.
31. English, *Spiritual Freedom*, p. 181.
32. Morris and Olsen, *Discerning God's Will Together*, p. 102.
33. Patricia Loring, *Spiritual Discernment: The Context and Goal of Clearness Committees* (Wallingford, PA: Pendle Hill Publications, 1992), p. 6.
34. Loring, *Listening Spirituality*, vol. 1, p. 74.
35. Albert Schweitzer, *Albert Schweitzer*, p. 72.
36. William A. Barry, *Finding God in All Things: A Companion to the Spiritual Exercises of St. Ignatius of Loyola* (Notre Dame: Ave Maria Press, 1991), p. 12.
37. M. Scott Peck, *People of the Lie: The Hope for Healing Human Evil* (New York: Touchstone, 1983), p. 10.
38. *The Life of St. Teresa of Jesus: Of the Order of Our Lady of Carmel, written by herself*, David Lewis trans. (Maryland: The Newman Bookshop, 1916), p. 260–262.
39. Marty Haugen, *Healer of Our Every Ill* (Chicago: G.I.A. Publications, 1991).
40. Steere, *Quaker Spirituality*, p. 42.
41. Anthony de Mello, *The Heart of the Enlightened* (New York: Doubleday, 1989), p. 159.
42. Mary Baker Eddy, *Science and Health: With Key to the Scriptures* (Boston: Christian Science Board of Directors, 1875), p. 107.
43. Sue Monk Kidd, *When the Heart Listens* (New York: HarperCollins, 1990), p. 43.
44. Michael Joncas, *On Eagle's Wings* (Portland: Oregon Catholic Press, 1979).
45. Evelyn Underhill, *The Essentials of Mysticism and Other Essays* (Oxford: Oneworld, 1999), p. 127.
46. Linnea Good, *The Sunday Sessions* (1994). Available at www.LinneaGood.com
47. Viktor Frankl, *Man's Search for Meaning* (New York: Simon and Schuster, 1985), p. 109.
48. Morris and Olsen, *Discerning God's Will Together*, p. 39.

Part 2: Methods
49. Coleman Barks with John Moyne, trans., *The Essential Rumi* (New York: HarperCollins Publishers, 1995), p. 114.
50. Thomas Merton, *The Seven Storey Mountain* (London: Sheldon Press, 1975), p. 206–207.
51. Fiona Bowie and Oliver Davies, eds., *Hildegard of Bingen: An Anthology* (London: SPCK, 1990), p. 91.

52. Kathryn Spink, *The Miracle of Love: Mother Teresa of Calcutta, Her Missionaries of Charity, and Her Co-Workers* (San Francisco: Harper & Row, 1981), p. 23.

53. Eddy, *Science and Health*, p. 11.

54. *Citadel of the Believer: Invocations from Qur'an and Sunnah* (Saudi Arabia: Darus-salam, 1997), p. 128–133

55. *Baha'i prayers: Holy writings*, p. 126.

56. The prayer "Rag Gauri," from *Guru Granth Sahib* (Amritsar, India: Hemkund Press, 1969), p. 262.

57. Eddy, *Science and Health*, p. 494.

58. Ted Dobson, *Say but the Word: How the Lord's Supper Can Transform Your Life* (Mahwah, NJ: Paulist Press, 1984), p. 23–24.

59. Loring, *Listening Spirituality*, vol. 2, p. 23.

60. Loring, *Listening Spirituality*, vol. 1, p. 13.

61. Wesley Kort, *"Take, Read": Scripture, Texuality and Cultural Practice* (University Park, PA: Pennsylvania State University Press, 1996), p. 21.

62. Louis Fischer, *Gandhi: His Life and Message for the World* (New York: New American Library, 1954), p. 30.

63. Barks with Moyne, *The Essential Rumi*, p. 15

64. English, *Spiritual Freedom*, p. 134.

65. Kelly Bulkeley, *Spiritual Dreaming: A Cross-cultural and Historical Journey* (Mahwah, NJ: Paulist Press, 1991), p. 3.

66. Murray Bodo, *The Way of St. Francis: The Challenge of Franciscan Spirituality for Everyone* (Cincinnati: St. Anthony Messenger Press, 1995), p. 5.

67. Justin Hayward, "A Question of Balance" from the album *The Moody Blues Greatest Hits* (1970).

68. English, *Spiritual Freedom*, p. 279.

69. Joseph Campbell with Bill Moyers, *The Power of Myth* (New York: Doubleday, 1988), p. 123.

70. Lauren Artress, *Walking a Sacred Path: Rediscovering the Labyrinth as a Spiritual Tool* (New York: Riverhead Books, 1995), p. xii.

71. Courtney Milne, *The Sacred Earth* (Middlesex, England: Viking, 1992), p. x.

72. Philip Cousineau, *The Art of Pilgrimage: The Seeker's Guide to Making Travel Sacred* (Berkeley, CA: Conari Press, 2000), p. xxiii.

73. Peace Pilgrim, *Her Life and Work*, p. 25.

74. Matsuo Basho, *Narrow Road to the Interior*, Sam Hamill, trans. (London: Shambhala, 1991), p. 58.

75. Huston Smith, *The World's Religions* (San Francisco: HarperCollins, 1991), p. 105.

76. Alcoholics Anonymous

77. Smith, *The World's Religions*, p. 105.

78. Saint Augustine, *The Confessions of St. Augustine*, John K. Ryan, trans. (New York: Doubleday and Co., 1960), pp. 234–5.

79. J. Philip Newell, *The Book of Creation: An Introduction to Celtic Spirituality* (Maywah, NJ: Paulist Press, 1999), p. 67–68.

80. Kabir Helminski, *The Knowing Heart: A Sufi Path of Transformation* (Boston: Shambhala, 2000), p. 270.

81. Cousineau, *The Art of Pilgrimage*, p. 161.

82. Alexander Eliot, *Earth, Air, Fire and Water* (New York: Simon & Schuster, 1962).

83. R. L. Wing, *The I Ching Workbook* (New York: Doubleday and Company, 1979), p. 42.

84. Carmen L. Caltagirone, *Friendship As Sacrament* (Staten Island: Alba House, 1989), p. 95.

85. Douglas V. Steere, *Gleanings: A Random Harvest* (Nashville: The Upper Room, 1986), p. 83.

86. Dyckman and Carroll, *Inviting the Mystic Supporting the Prophet*, p. 20.

87. Thomas N. Hart, *The Art of Christian Listening* (Mahwah, NJ: Paulist Press, 1980), p. 161.

88. English, *Spiritual Freedom*, p. 3.

89. Jean Vanier, *Becoming Human* (Toronto: House of Anansi Press Limited, 1998), pp. 128–130.

90. The Qur'an (Sura 98.1–5) as quoted in Paul Varo Martinson, ed., *Islam: An Introduction for Christians* (Minneapolis: Augsburg, 1994).

91. Martinson, *Islam: An Introduction for Christians*, p. 44.

92. English, *Spiritual Freedom*, p. 294.

93. *Advices and Queries*, published proceedings of the yearly meeting of the Religious Society of Friends (Quakers) in Britain, 1995, p. 12.

94. Parker Palmer, *Let Your Life Speak: Listening for the Voice of Vocation* (San Francisco: Jossey-Bass, 2000), pp. 45–46.

95. Morris and Olsen, *Discerning God's Will Together*, p. 11.

96. Wuellner, *Heart of Healing Heart of Light*, p. 99.

97. Dyckman and Carroll, *Inviting the Mystic Supporting the Prophet*, p. 61.

98. Daniel Schutte, "Here I Am Lord," (Portland: Oregon Catholic Press, 1981).

99. Pat Bergen, CSJ, *Holy Wisdom*, Ministry of the Arts, Sisters of St. Joseph of LaGrange, IL, 2000.

Suggested Reading & Resources

Besides those books already listed in the endnotes, I highly recommend the following titles.

General

Bradley, Ian. *Celtic Christian Communities: Live the Tradition.* Northstone, 2000.

Bromiley, Geoffrey W. *Theological Dictionary of the New Testament.* Grand Rapids: William B. Erdmans Publishing Co., 1985.

Buber, Martin. *Eclipse of God.* New York: Harper and Brothers, 1952.

— . *Tales of the Hasidim: The Early Masters.* New York: Schocken, 1947.

— . *Tales of the Hasidim: The Later Masters.* New York: Schocken, 1948.

Caldwell, Erin. *Angels & Oranges.* Saltspring Island: Alandra-Vtral, 1995.

French, R. M., trans. *The Way of a Pilgrim.* San Francisco: Harper Collins, 1965.

Hawker, Paul. *Secret Affairs of the Soul: Ordinary People's Extraordinary Experiences of the Sacred.* Northstone, 2000.

— . *Soul Survivor: A Spiritual Quest through 40 Days and 40 Nights of Mountain Solitude.* Northstone, 1998.

Johnston, William. *The Inner Eye of Love: Mysticism and Religion.* New York: Harper & Row Publishers Inc., 1978.

LaBerge, S. *Lucid Dreaming.* Los Angeles: J. P. Tarcher, 1985.

LaBerge, Stephen and Howard Rheingold. *Exploring the World of Lucid Dreaming.* New York: Ballantine Books, 1990.

Mark, Barbara and Trudy Griswold. *Angelspeake: How to Talk with Your Angels.* New York: Simon & Schuster, 1995.

Outlaw, Maxine. *Pray Like Hell: How to Talk with God.* Kansas City: Andrews & McMeel, 1998.

Popov, Linda Kavelin. *Sacred Moments: Daily Meditations on the Virtues.* New York: Penguin Putnam Inc., 1996.

Progoff, Ira, trans. *The Cloud of Unknowing.* New York: Delta, 2000.

Sheldrake, Philip. *Befriending Our Desires.* Montreal: Novalis, 2001.

Spivak, Dawnine. *Grass Sandals: The Travels of Basho.* New York: Athenium Books, 1977.

Wright, Keith. *Religious Abuse: A Pastor Explores the Many Ways Religion Can Hurt as well as Heal.* Northstone, 2001.

Spiritual practices

Chittister, Joan D. *Heart of Flesh: A Feminist Spirituality for Women and Men.* Grand Rapids: William B. Eerdmans, 1998.

Dalai Lama. *The Art of Happiness.* New York: Penguin/Putnam, 2000.

Hurst, Viki. *Personal Pilgrimage: One Day Soul Journeys for Busy People.* Northstone, 2000.

Spiritual personal growth

Kurtz, Ernest and Katherine Ketchem. *The Spirituality of Imperfection: Storytelling and the Journey to Wholeness*. NY: Bantam Books, 1992.

Kushner, Harold S. *How Good Do We Have To Be? A New Understanding of Guilt and Forgiveness*. Boston: Little Brown and Co., 1996.

Popov, Linda Kavelin et al. *The Family Virtues Guide: Simple Ways to Bring Out the Best in Our Children and Ourselves*. New York: Plume, 1997.

Rupp, Joyce. *Dear Heart Come Home: The Path of Mid-life Spirituality*. New York: Crossroad, 1996.

Wiederkehr, Macrina. *Behold Your Life: A Pilgrimage through Your Memories*. Notre Dame: Ave Maria Press, 2000.

Healing

Graham, Rochelle, Flora Litt, and Wayne Irwin. *Healing from the Heart. A Guide to Christian Healing for Individuals and Groups*. Wood Lake Books, 1998.

Harpur, Tom. *The Uncommon Touch: An Investigation of Spiritual Healing*. Toronto: McClelland & Steward, 1994.

Reeves, Nancy. *A Path through Loss: A Guide to Writing Your Healing and Growth*. Kelowna: Northstone, 2001.

Wuellner, Flora Slosson. *Release: Healing from Wounds of Family, Church, and Community*. Nashville: Upper Room Books, 1996.

Discernment

Barry, William A. *Paying Attention to God: Discernment in Prayer*. Notre Dame: Ave Maria Press, 1990.

Conroy, Maureen. *The Discerning Heart: Discovering a Personal God*. Chicago: Loyola University Press, 1993.

Morris, Danny E. *Yearning to Know God's Will: A Workbook for Discerning God's Guidance for Your Life*. Grand Rapids: Zondervan, 1991.

Retreat centers

Hughes J. J. & V. D. *Overnight and Short Stay at Religious Houses Around the World* (5th ed.). Bloomfield, NJ: Hugen Press, 1995.

Jones, Timothy. *A Place for God: A Guide to Spiritual Retreats and Retreat Centers*. New York: Doubleday, 2000.

Kelly, M. and J. *Sanctuaries: The Northeast* [U.S.] New York: Bell Tower, 1993.

Kelly, M. and J. *Sanctuaries: The West Coast and Southwest* [U.S.] New York: Bell Tower, 1993.

Regalbuto, R. J. *A Guide to Monastic Guest Houses*. 3rd ed. U.S. and Canada. Ridgefield, CT: Morehouse Publishing, 1998.

Retreats International, P.O. Box 1067, Notre Dame, IN USA 46556
Ph: 219-631-5320 Fax: 219-631-4546
E-mail: RETREATS.RETREATS.1@nd.edu
Web: www.retreatsintl.org

Art and song
If you can't find the art or music referred to in the text in your local stores, contact:

Colleen Fulmer – available in the free Heartbeats catalogue, a "venture advocacy" ministry of the Sisters of the Humility of Mary, Cleveland, Ohio. The catalogue provides advertising space for women, groups in developing countries, and minority artists. 1-800-808-1991 in U.S. or 440-356-8601 www.en.com/users/heartbt

Linnea Good – available via her web site: www.LinneaGood.com

Cover art by *Sr. Mary Southard* and the discernment blessing by *Sr. Pat Bergen* is in the Ministry of the Arts (M.O.T.A.) catalogue available free at 1-800-354-3504. M.O.T.A. is a ministry of the Sisters of St. Joseph of La Grange, Ill. The catalogue includes music tapes, cards, and sculpture.

Enneagram
The Enneagram Institute, New York, NY. Don Riso and Russ Hudson. (212) 932-3306. www.enneagraminstitute.com.

Center for Action and Contemplation, Richard Rohr, OFM. Albuquerque, NM (505) 242-9588, www.cacradicalgrace.org. Retreat center and puts out the newspaper *Radical Grace*.

Index